DEATHTRAPS

DEATHTRAPS

THE POSTMODERN COMEDY THRILLER

Marvin Carlson

INDIANA UNIVERSITY PRESS • Bloomington and Indianapolis

The paper used in this publication meets the minimum requirements of American National Standard for Information Sciences—Permanence of Paper for Printed Library Materials, ANSI Z39.48-1984.

 ™

Manufactured in the United States of America

Library of Congress Cataloging-in-Publication Data

Carlson, Marvin A., date.
    Deathtraps : the postmodern comedy thriller / Marvin Carlson.
      p.   cm.
    Includes bibliographical references and index.
    ISBN 0-253-31305-8 (alk. paper). — ISBN 0-253-20826-2 (alk. paper)
    1. Detective and mystery plays, English—History and criticism.
    2. Detective and mystery plays, American—History and criticism.
    3. American drama—20th century—History and criticism.   4. English drama—20th century—History and criticism.   5. American drama (Comedy)—History and criticism.   6. English drama (Comedy)—History and criticism.   7. Postmodernism (Literature)—Great Britain.
8. Postmodernism (Literature)—United States.   I. Title.
PR739.D48C36   1993
822'.052709—dc20   92-45237

1 2 3 4 5 97 96 95 94 93

To Crystal Matthews
and all that she represents

CONTENTS

WARNING TO THE READER

The effectiveness of the plays considered in this book depends to a great extent upon surprise. The programs of *Sleuth* specially noted "for the enjoyment of future audiences, it would be greatly appreciated if you would not disclose the plot of this play." At the curtain call for *Accomplice* an actor similarly enjoined the audience to silence on the play's many surprises, and advertising for that production included the phrase "The show that everybody's NOT talking about." Since a good deal of the effect of the traditional detective drama depends on the surprise of the ending, and a good deal of the modern comedy thriller depends on other surprises, there is a long tradition of silence in the theatre concerning the plot devices and endings of such plays to protect the pleasure of potential viewers. This silence is perhaps most notably observed (although almost invariably with ironic comment) by newspaper reviewers who are bound by this convention not to speak specifically of what is usually the most striking and distinctive feature of the work they are reviewing. Since it is precisely the workings of these devices that this study considers, however, it must necessarily break this convention of silence. The reader is warned that major surprises in a number of modern thrillers are herein revealed. Those who have not yet seen or read these plays and who wish to preserve their innocence, should read no further than the general introduction. The dates given in the text are normally those of production. Publication dates will be found in note citations.

DEATHTRAPS

1 THE BUSINESS OF MURDER

"Some people believe that murder is an art, sir."
—Stenning in *Murderer*

When the term *postmodern* is encountered in the contemporary American theatre, it is almost invariably found in the rather rarefied world of experimental and avant-garde performance. The term has been applied to most of the central examples of the current avant-garde, such as the Wooster Group, the Mabou Mines, Richard Foreman, and the performance artists collectively known as the New Vaudevillians.[1] Despite a great variety of approaches, all of these groups share a number of concerns often identified with postmodern artistic expression, among them the interrelated techniques of self-referentiality, foregrounding of the work in process, and calculated disruption of those codes anticipated by the reader/audience.

The fusing of such concerns with the apparatus of modern technology has given many of the productions of these and similar groups a very contemporary edge. However, the concerns themselves have long been associated with the theatrical avant-garde, for so long, in fact, that they have themselves entered into what might be called, somewhat paradoxically, the mainstream tradition of the twentieth-century avant-garde in theatre. In many European countries this avant-garde has also become an important part of the major theatre tradition, if not in the commercial theatre, then certainly in the state theatres of France, Germany, and elsewhere, which in these countries constitutes the theatrical mainstream.

The situation is very different in England and America. In these countries the major dramatic tradition, represented primarily by productions in London's West End and at the national theatres and in America by Broadway and the major regional theatres, has remained throughout the century strongly oriented toward realism and the general approach laid out a century ago by such dramatists as Ibsen (in his middle period), Chekhov, and Shaw. This tradition has proven remarkably resistant to alteration. A few dramatists, most notably Wilder and Pirandello, have achieved a continuing modest success outside this tradition, but they have inspired almost no important imitators, and other major non-realistic dramatists, such as Strindberg, Brecht, or Beckett, have never really established themselves on major English or American commercial stages.

During the last two decades, however, the works produced in one specific and seemingly quite unlikely genre of the major commercial theatre in England and America have regularly and strikingly eroded the conventions and expectations of realism with a kind of postmodern playfulness. Such activities have now entered the expectations of the genre, surely the only place where they are yet to be found in the mainstream English-language theatre. There is no generally accepted generic name for the type of play involved, though regular theatre-goers in New York, and even more in London, will instantly recognize it as a familiar type of offering. The subject of the play is murder, planned or already committed, and the action is the successful or unsuccessful efforts of the murderer to prevent his or her exposure. The most common name for such plays, especially in England, is thrillers. Earlier in the century, these dramas were called melodramas or mystery plays. Others more recently have been called plays or comedies of suspense, still others just plays.

The play that has an unsolved murder as its central concern has, of course, a long and honored history in Western drama, headed by two of the most revered classics of that tradition, *Oedipus* and *Hamlet*. In more recent times, however, the murder drama has attracted very little attention from either historians or theorists, even though almost every season throughout this century has produced examples of the murder drama on the stages of London and New York and even though the best known example of the genre, Agatha Christie's *The Mousetrap* (1952), has become the longest running play in the history of the theatre. The complicated development of the modern thriller has still to be traced and will not be undertaken here, but some of the outlines of its history need to be suggested in order to form a basis for an understanding of the radical developments in this genre during the past two decades.

The modern mystery thriller's history is closely intertwined with that of the detective novel. Conan Doyle himself adapted his short story *The Speckled Band* for the stage, and William Gillette built a play, and indeed a career, around Doyle's immortal Sherlock Holmes. Later Mary Roberts Rinehart, Edgar Wallace, and of course Agatha Christie, among many others, created stage mysteries after establishing themselves as mystery novelists. Not surprisingly, these authors and their public often found the stage offerings rather thin compared with the more detailed narrative possibilities offered by the novel. Most would quite reverse the opinion of Dorothy Sayers, who is reported to have said that the adaptation of *Busman's Honeymoon* as a novel contained only the "limbs and outward flourishes" of the original stage version.[2] Thus the many recent studies of mystery and detective fiction, when they speak of the theatrical thriller at all, tend to consider it as little more than a rather minor derivative form, capitalizing on the success of other detective fiction.

In fact, however, the mystery play has a background dating

back at least as far as and in some cases drawing upon rather different traditions from that of the mystery novel. Crime—especially murder, mystery, and suspense—has been a staple of the mystery drama since the plays of Ancient Greece, but the more immediate background for the modern mystery drama clearly lies in the popular melodrama of the nineteenth century and the English Gothic dramas and pantomime dialogues that fed into this tradition. Crime is so central a topic to this tradition that the Boulevard du Temple in Paris, where the melodrama houses were concentrated in the early nineteenth century, was more commonly called the "Boulevard du Crime." The crime presented was of many sorts, from the exotic and hallucinatory tradition of the Gothic, with its ruined castles, creaking doors, flashes of lightning, and ghostly phenomena, to the bloody realism of stage works based on contemporary murders, long the subject matter of popular balladeers. The melodrama houses of England offered very similar fare (indeed sometimes the same fare in pirated versions), so that the popular Victoria Theatre, for example, was affectionately referred to by its patrons as "The Bleedin' Vic." Rather exotic mystery drama was the more common American fare in the early years of the century, but by the 1820s and 1830s real life murder stories, such as Maria Marten's death in the infamous Red Barn or the exploits of the "demon barber" Sweeney Todd were much more in vogue.

Many of the atmospheric elements and devices for creating tension and suspense in the modern thriller can be traced directly back to the Gothic melodrama and its variations, while the specific attention to the mechanics of the crime itself owes much to "true-crime" plays such as the many versions of the Maria Marten story. Yet the typical crime melodrama of the early nineteenth century still differed in a number of important respects from the typical murder mystery of a century later, not least in the depiction of the two pivotal antagonists—the murderer-villain and the detective-hero. In Ordean A. Haugen's entertaining encyclopedia of crime fiction, *Who Done It* (1969), the section on "Mystery Plays" begins:

> Suddenly the lights go out, and there is a hushed silence. Then a shot breaks the quiet of the night, followed by a harrowing scream. When the lights come on, a body lies in full view of the audience. Now they can breathe easier again, sit back and relax. The show is on.[3]

The entire organization of the action may well be as predictable as this typical opening. The often rather isolated setting where the murder has occurred will shelter a number of characters, one of them, preferably the least likely one, the unknown murderer. A detective arrives and after shrewd cross-examination, observance of clues, careful comparison of alibis, and/or reconstruction of the crime, announces in the final moments of the play the identity of the murderer. The centrality of this quest and unmasking is suggested by the common sobriquet for such narratives: a "whodunnit."

The murderer in the melodramas and crime plays of the early nineteenth century played no such retiring role. He or she was known to the audience from the beginning, and his or her evil plots, deeds, even thoughts (through asides and monologues) were clearly, indeed lavishly, displayed to the audience. Although some representative of the law might be needed at the conclusion to bring the villain to justice (like the Bow Street Runner who arrests Corder in *Maria Marten*), there was little need for a detective figure in such plays because there was no hidden crime to detect. Detectives did, however, begin to appear as major characters by the 1820s, largely under the influence of the *Mémoires* of the first Parisian chief of detectives, François Vidocq, published in 1820. Like their French model, these detectives were a rather rough-and-tumble lot, not much better morally than the ruffians they pursued and much more adept at disguise and bluff than at processes of ratiocination. The most famous of these characters is surely the beloved Hawkshaw in

Tom Taylor's 1863 *The Ticket-of-Leave Man*, whose name remained almost proverbial throughout the rest of the century.

The same year as Taylor's *Ticket-of-Leave Man*, a popular play in Paris, *L'Aïeule*, anticipated far more exactly the concerns and the structure of the later murder thriller. It was in fact adapted by Taylor the following year as *The Hidden Hand*. *L'Aïeule*, like many such plays, was not an original story, and it already had a complicated stage history when it was adapted by the popular melodrama team of Edmond and Dennery. The story is based (very loosely) upon *Die Ahnfrau*, the first play of the Austrian dramatist Franz Grillparzer and also the first of a genre of popular romantic drama in Germany called Fate Tragedies. Offered in Vienna in 1817, it had already inspired adaptations in London and New York when Edmond and Dennery saw in it an idea that could be reworked along lines suggested by the tales of Edgar Allan Poe, which were extremely popular in mid-century Paris.

In both the English and French versions of this drama, a beautiful young girl in a feudal castle is slowly wasting away and one of the guests in the castle, anticipating Sherlock Holmes and many later sleuths, secretly analyzes the girl's drinking water and finds poison in it (arsenic in the English version). During the course of the action various members of the family and of the castle entourage arouse suspicion, but the poisoner is still unknown in the final scene, when the threatened girl has announced her plans to leave the castle and all the suspects are assembled for a police investigation. The girl asks for a drink of water, but her younger niece, who suspects the real poisoner, seizes and starts to drink it. The old grandmother, a supposed paralytic, leaps up to stop her, revealing herself as the villain. She drinks the potion and dies.

Despite the success of these plays (and of an American version, *The Grey Lady of Penarvon*, in 1865), the detective and crime plays of the later nineteenth century, and these were numerous and popular, did not often involve this sort of audience mystification. Even when such novels of mystery as Wilkie Collins's *The Moonstone* and *The Woman in White* were adapted for the theatre in the 1870s, much of the suspense of the originals disappeared, apparently due to a feeling that theatre audiences were less sophisticated than readers and needed clearer explanations. The critic Dutton Cook, for example, approved the Collins changes, observing that readers could be mystified to almost any extent, while in the theatre it was "advisable to enlighten a spectator concerning the secrets of a plot at the earliest possible opportunity."[4] Even the famous *Sherlock Holmes* of William Gillette (1899) emphasized suspense and surprise rather than mystery, and a loose episodic plot with much action rather than ratiocination.

In the early years of the twentieth century, a group of New York dramatists, most of them trained in the tradition of melodrama, began to develop a more concentrated type of mystery drama, one in which a murder is committed at or before the beginning of the play and suspicion falls upon a number of characters before the "detective," usually not a policeman, reveals the true murderer at the end of the action, often through some psychological entrapment. There is usually a single setting, either the scene of the crime, in which case the murder is often shown, or a courtroom, portraying the subsequent trial. The scene of the crime very frequently recalls the Gothic forerunners of this genre. A mysterious country house with secret panels, creaking stairs, occasional flashes of lightning, and a suggestion (always incorrect) of possible occult forces share the stage with the rationality of detection in such early and highly popular examples of the genre as Bayard Veiller's *The Thirteenth Chair* (1916) or John Willard's *The Cat and the Canary* (1922), and continue in the popular Agatha Christie works of the next generation. Despite such Gothic touches, extremely careful plotting, subtle dialogue, and greater attention to character psychology in these plays replaced the traditional crime and detective drama's reliance upon action and spectacle, leading one of the first specialists in such drama, Owen Davis, to insist that the form was "a very exact and exacting one," calling for "more technical skill and inventive power than any other form of play making."[5]

The success of American mysteries of the teens and twenties in London, along with the growing popularity of the mystery novel thanks to authors like G. K. Chesterton and Agatha Christie, stimulated an interest in such work among English dramatists. Several of the first and best of these works utilized a device that would decline in popularity during the flowering of the genre in the 1930s and 1940s but which would reappear as a central feature in the new comedy thrillers of the 1970s and 1980s. This device is to actually show the crime committed early in the play, so that the audience is in no doubt about the murderer's identity, but also to have the murderer develop and perhaps rehearse an elaborate alibi, so that the subsequent tension results from wondering whether the scheme will work. Patrick Hamilton's *Rope* in 1929 and Anthony Armstrong's *Ten-minute Alibi* in 1933 were particularly striking examples of this approach. Hamilton's play was subsequently the basis for one of Alfred Hitchcock's most admired films, *Rope,* and the murder plot and complex alibi-gone-wrong recur in a number of Hitchcock films, perhaps most memorably in *Dial M for Murder,* based on an English television and stage play by Frederick Knott.

During the 1930s and 1940s the classic detective story reached its apogee in the works of such authors as Christie, Dorothy L. Sayers, John Dickson Carr, and Ellery Queen. During these same years, the detective drama was also becoming a standard feature of the English-language stage, though its real blossoming came somewhat later, in the 1940s and 1950s. Agatha Christie, the only major author of mystery novels to become also a major author of mystery dramas, dominated the genre, offering at least one new play in eleven of the fifteen seasons between 1944 and 1960 and often having several plays running concurrently. Although an average of five or six new "thrillers" appeared each season on the London stage from 1952 onward, no other dramatist in this genre approached Christie either in the number of works offered or in the popularity of her most successful dramas. Although Christie achieved this success with both "scene of the crime" dramas like *The Mousetrap* and with courtroom dramas like *Witness for the Prosecution*, it was the former model that proved most popular, most imitated by other dramatists, and, not surprisingly, the major target of Tom Stoppard's witty parody of the genre in 1968, *The Real Inspector Hound*.

The very solidity and predictability of generic codes in a genre like detective fiction make it a tempting target for the foregrounding or dismantling of those codes that is the basis of parody. In this sense, Stoppard's work is very much in the tradition of such famous theatre parodies as Villiers's *The Rehearsal* or Fielding's *Tom Thumb* (indeed the National Theatre stressed this historical parallel by offering a delightful double bill of Sheridan's *The Critic* and *The Real Inspector Hound* in 1986). Like most of Stoppard's works, however, *The Real Inspector Hound* plays with epistemological and ontological questions that go far beyond its parodic surface and make it a kind of forerunner of a group of equally subversive mystery dramas from the early 1970s onward. In these dramas, the parodic element is much less central and the total effect seems even closer to the enterprise that in other contexts has been characterized as postmodern.

The operations of parody are already very close to those of postmodernist expression. Indeed Linda Hutcheon has argued that parody is in some senses the perfect postmodern form, "for it paradoxically both incorporates and challenges that which it parodies."[6] The important concept here is not the specific goal of parody, however, but its particular double mode of operation. Hutcheon sees in this double mode the most marked distinction between postmodernism and the avant-garde. Although the two approaches share some experimental techniques, their relationship to previous, especially mainstream, work is quite different. While the avant-garde defines itself by opposition, postmodernism simultaneously exalts and questions conventional procedures. It "uses and abuses, installs and then subverts, the very concepts it challenges."[7]

A useful term that describes the simultaneous celebration and subversion of conventional expectations that characterizes postmodernism is *double-coding*, utilized by Charles Jencks in his analyses of postmodern architecture. According to Jencks, double-coding develops the play of paradox that seeks to encourage in the public an openness in receptive strategies and a consciousness of the constructedness of the expression. In architecture, this strategy is particularly apparent in structures that are half-modernist, half-conventional, with each half serving as a playful destabilization of the absolutist claims of the other.[8]

In postmodernist expression, popular and familiar art forms often provide particularly attractive material for development. The modern detective drama might at first thought seem hardly the most promising site for the eruption of avant-garde experimentation into mainstream theatre, but postmodern experimentation is quite a different matter. The simultaneous celebration and subversion of conventional procedures outlined by Hutcheon and Jencks is a process particularly suited to a highly and clearly codified genre of this sort, with its extremely predictable rules of construction and expectations (so strong as almost to amount to rules) of its type of setting, characters, character relationships, dialogue, and so on. The distinctly popular, not literary, background of the genre is by no means a disadvantage either, since the playing of the avant-garde dynamics of high culture against the conventionalized expectations of a popular cultural form is also a favored postmodernist strategy. .

Spanos and Tani[9] have in fact argued that detective fiction is, among such popular forms as the Western, the fantasy, or the romance, particularly attractive to postmodernist explorations, concerned as it commonly is with "undermining the detective-like expectations of the positivistic mind."[10] This assertion is strongly supported by the importance of this popular tradition in the work of such postmodern authors as Jorge Luis Borges, Umberto Eco, and Paul Auster,[11] where we find precisely the fulfillment of and simultaneous challenge to the familiar existing generic codes of traditional detective fiction.

In theatrical theory, the concept of double-coding has particularly been associated with the tension between theatrical text and performance. Josette Féral, for example, has argued that "theatricality" arises from the dynamic interplay of these two. Theatre inscribes the subject in the symbolic, in "theatrical codes," while performance undoes codes and competencies, deconstructing those systems established by theatre. The interworking of these two creates a field of continuous displacement and endless play.[12] More recently, Michael Vanden Heuvel has specifically tied this theatrical dialectic to Jencks's concepts. Like contemporary architecture, Heuvel suggests, recent theatre has adopted a kind of "adhocism," which characteristically "double-codes" or consciously juxtaposes elements, idioms, and functions "to create ironic and transformative space between them." Most commonly in the recent theatre, Heuvel says, this double-coding has been "built upon an open-ended and speculative relationship between the dramatic text and its claims to objectivity, its human reference, and its satisfying sense of closure on the one hand, and the emphasis on interiority, deconstructive dispersal, and liminality inherent to performance on the other."[13] Although Heuvel focuses upon such central figures of the modern avant-garde as the Wooster Group, Robert Wilson, Samuel Beckett, and Sam Shepard, the double-coding based on the ironic juxtaposition of traditional goal-directed narrative and the instability of performance can also clearly be seen in the recent works of the more commercial and mainstream thriller tradition. Very often the major destabilizing force in these works is the foregrounding of a performance consciousness, either metaphorically, as the characters construct and play roles within the fiction, or more recently, literally, as the audience is called upon to recognize a clear disjuncture between the fictive world of the narrative and the actors who may or may not carry out the presumed imperatives of that world.

Many of the tricks and devices found in the particularly subversive new detective dramas of the 1970s and 1980s plays were not new, but their combination in theatrical productions that emphasized such postmodern concerns as self-reflexivity, epistemological incertitude, and subversion of traditional codes (both within the performance and governing its relationship with the audience) not only provided a distinctly new orientation in this familiar genre, but also offered a kind of experimentation rarely, if ever, encountered elsewhere in the mainstream theatre of this period, especially in England and America. The first major success of this new approach, and in many ways a model for those that followed, was Anthony Shaffer's *Sleuth* in 1970. A murder plot, a victim, a police inspector, and a murder investigation—all the standard features of the conventional detective story are present, and yet not one of them is what it seems. Each of the conventional generic codings the audience can be expected to make is subverted and the subversion itself utilized, not to make fun of the genre, as in Stoppard, but to fulfill its conventional goal of shocking and surprising the audience by unconventional means that, as Hutcheon claims for postmodern practice, "use and abuse, install and then subvert" the machinery of the genre itself. The success of the drama as well as its unconventionality was echoed in the reviews, the great majority of which both praised its originality and hinted at its subversion. Significantly, the one clearly negative review, by Martin Gottfried, of the New York production was negative precisely because of *Sleuth*'s subversion of the "rules." "I have never been a big reader of mysteries," Gottfried admitted, "but I am aware that they rest on a cornerstone of logic. *Sleuth* is alogical from the start." "Another rule of mysteries," he continued, "is that the reader (or in the case of a play, the spectator) has to be given all the clues. . . . Still another rule is that you cannot constantly fool the reader (audience) with the same device. The third time around, one isn't fooled as much as irritated. The appeal of a mystery is in piecing out the puzzle, not wondering when (if ever) a feint will become an action."[14]

The standard Gottfried is applying to *Sleuth* is very much that of the "fair-play rule" articulated by Dorothy L. Sayers in her "Author's Note" to *Busman's Honeymoon* in 1936:

> The rule is that every clue must be shown at the same time to the public and to the detective, so that both have an equal chance to solve the problem. The public must not be told the secret of the crime beforehand; nor must the detective acquire any private information which he does not immediately impart to the public.[15]

What Gottfried failed to realize was that *Sleuth* represented a different sort of mystery play (indeed Sayers herself distinguished the "detective problem play" from the "thriller" precisely on the basis of the "fair-play rule"), in which logic is *not* the cornerstone, but indeed is consciously destabilized, in which the spectator does not get "all the clues," in which the goal is indeed to constantly fool the audience by fair means or foul, and where the appeal is precisely not in "piecing out the puzzle" but in "wondering when (if ever) a feint will become an action." In short, *Sleuth* was a mystery play of instability and of playful self-consciousness. In such a work, the game is no longer to match wits with the detective in the solving of a crime, but to engage in a playful and highly self-conscious dismantling of the dramatic universe. Gottfried's complaint that *Sleuth* was "both a mystery and a parody of one, mocking the cliches and mechanics of detective stories while capitalizing on them," while meant as a criticism, comes remarkably close to the workings of postmodernism described by Hutcheon or Jencks.

Fortunately most critics and audiences in 1970 had less trouble than Gottfried in dealing with the double-coding of *Sleuth*

and recognizing that its attraction lay precisely in its simultaneous acknowledgment and subversion of conventional generic
expectations. *Sleuth* won the Tony award for the best New York
play of the season and proved an enormous success in London,
New York, and indeed around the world. This success opened
the way for a series of similar works in New York and London.
Christie's indestructible *Mousetrap* continued to run in London
(as it continues today), but after 1970, new mystery plays were
at least as likely to follow *Sleuth* in the postmodernist mode of
simultaneously building up and subverting the familiar conventions of the mystery drama as follow *The Mousetrap* in the more
straightforward reformulation of those conventions championed
by Gottfried. Precisely what to call these plays remains a bit of
a problem. The term *comedy thriller*, particularly in America,
seems to be gaining in popularity, and this term seems quite
appropriate, not only because such plays are indeed often comedic in their repartee, but on a more profound level, in their
playful subversion of traditional generic expectations. *Accomplice*
(1991), a recent and particularly well-developed example of the
genre, uses the designation of comedy thriller, and an author's
note to Gerald Moon's *Corpse!* (1985) insists specifically that "in
all advertising and publicity no description other than 'Comedy
thriller' may be used."[16]

Anthony Shaffer contributed two other important works to
this new subgenre, *Murderer* in 1975 and *Whodunnit* in 1982, but
the other best known example of this sort of play is probably
Ira Levin's *Deathtrap* in 1978. No play of this type during the
1980s achieved the success or reputation of *Sleuth* or *Deathtrap*,
but the subgenre remained popular, with at least one strong
new example, and often more, available each season. The complexity and the intensity of the generic subversion steadily increased also, since a new sort of game was being played with
the audience. In the traditional "whodunnit," the audience was
provided with a murder and a collection of possible suspects
and the game was a simple one. The author sought to mislead

expectations and at the end reveal the murderer as someone whom, ideally, the audience should have suspected, but did not. In the new thrillers, the game is far more complex. The playwright constantly seeks to surprise the audience about any, and every, aspect of the dramatic construction, and to this all-encompassing game, anything may be sacrificed, including, sometimes most notably, the rules of the genre itself. The character of Clifford, a young, would-be writer of thrillers, in a typically self-reflexive passage from *Deathtrap*, speaks of the lure and the challenge of this genre:

> . . . it's a tradition: a superbly challenging theatrical framework in which every possible variation seems to have been played. Can I conjure up a few new ones? Can I startle an audience that's *been* on Angel Street, that's dialed "M" for murder, that's witnessed the prosecution, that's played the murder game.[17]

As Clifford realizes, and as *Deathtrap* itself stunningly illustrates, a genre dedicated to surprising audiences with unexpected turns inevitably finds audiences becoming more and more difficult to take off guard. On the other hand, they also become open to more and more radical and complex subversion of expectations. The result is a machine for increasing destabilization of generic givens and creating their replacement by ludic experimentation. Not long after the appearance of such new style comedy thrillers as *Sleuth*, a little one-act parody, David Fulk's *The Potman Spoke Sooth* (1977), seized upon precisely this tendency toward experimentation in such plays and offered an amusing exploration of what might become of a mystery drama when every basis of grounding or authority was systemically removed.

The Potman was essentially a modest *jeu d'esprit* seeking, in the parody tradition, only to amuse by exaggerating elements in a popular form. Still, it in fact anticipated developments in the main line of the genre it was parodying, much as Stoppard's more substantial *The Real Inspector Hound* had done almost a decade before. The play of illusion and reality became even more central and more complex in such comedy thrillers of the 1980s as *The Butler Did It* (1981), Shaffer's *Whodunnit* (1982), Nick Hall's *Dead Wrong* (1985) and John Pielmeier's *Sleight of Hand* (1988), and there is often specific playing with the conventions of the theatre as well as the conventions of mystery fiction in a more open and self-conscious manner than was seen in the comedy thrillers of the previous decade. In a recent (1990) example of this genre on Broadway, Rupert Holmes's *Accomplice*, the techniques of subversion have moved to a central position in every aspect of the work—its organization, performance, and reception. In a later chapter, I will offer a detailed analysis of this production, the most fully developed example yet of a comedy thriller that might be even more accurately termed a postmodern detective play.

Certainly, as *The Potman* slyly suggests and *Deathtrap* specifically proposes, the requirement of finding ever new ways to surprise audiences has undoubtedly helped to fuel the recent development of this strange subgenre, but this is hardly a sufficient explanation for the emergence and popularity of the modern comedy thriller. Were more conventional approaches truly exhausted, few if any new works in those more conventional styles would be appearing or finding audiences, but in fact new examples of traditional mystery dramas continue to appear on the stages of New York and London. If their number is distinctly less than during the golden years of the 1940s and 1950s (when indeed more live commercial theatre of every type was available) the field of mystery novels is at present so lively that many speak of a new golden age, and the great majority of these novels still closely follow traditional approaches.

The particular type of experimentation undertaken in the comedy thrillers might suggest, to those familiar only with the mystery tradition, the last mannerist elaborations of a nearly exhausted form. An awareness of the sorts of activity in other artistic fields to which the general name of *postmodernism* has been given, however, suggests that the creators of these contemporary dramas are responding at least as much to a general cultural consciousness as they are to the specific demands of their own field. The great intellectual systems, scientific and philosophical, that provided a meaningful grounding for human thought and activity through the last century have been widely challenged in recent times by writers in a wide variety of disciplines, perhaps most notably in physics and philosophy. Werner Heisenberg, in his highly influential *Physics and Philosophy* (1962), argued that the epistemological and ontological uncertainty introduced to the world of physics by quantum theory and relativity theory must inevitably affect the world of philosophy as well. Indeed not only philosophy, but most areas of the arts and humanities have in recent years seemed to provide evidence of this. Looking specifically at the modern experimental theatre, Natalie Crohn Schmitt, in her *Actors and Onlookers* (1990), does not argue for a specific influence of the modern scientific thought on such theatre, but suggests that the two clearly inhabit the same intellectual world, where the ambiguous, aleatory compositions of an artist like John Cage seem a more appropriate reflection of reality than the logical, predictable forms of the Aristotelian tradition.

Similarly, it is not likely that the creators or the audiences of modern comedy thrillers are particularly aware in any specific detail of the issues involved in postmodern theory. For most of them, postmodern is probably not much more than a fashionable and rather vague contemporary cultural term. Nevertheless, these creators and audiences are a part of the same general culture as quantum physicists, postmodern theorists, and for that matter, consciously experimental theatre groups, and the intellectual and cultural consciousness of these theatre artists and audiences is subject to many of the same general tensions and preoccupations. The comedy thriller, however, seems to reflect certain techniques and concerns of the postmodern more directly and consistently than do many other popular subgenres of literature and theatre. This I would suggest is because, as a genre, it possesses certain features that make it particularly well suited for reflecting these techniques and concerns.

Silvio Gaggi in his study of postmodern art has taken the theatre as his model typological system, since he sees in the theatre particularly well-developed explorations of modes of self-referentiality, a strategy he develops as central to postmodern art.[18] I shall return later to his use of Pirandello and Brecht as models for different modes of self-referentiality, but will note here that the modern comedy thriller is particularly rich in utilization of this technique so that it might be quite properly considered a distinguishing feature of this genre, as Gaggi and others have argued that it is of postmodern expression in general. Beyond this important technical feature, however, the general and specific subject matter of the comedy thriller allies it closely to the concerns of the postmodern. The situation of the comedy thriller as a genre developed in specific opposition to the classic detective drama with its championing of a positivistic world view has already been mentioned. This opposition allies the comedy thriller closely with the skepticism found throughout postmodern expression concerning such traditional grounding signifiers as individual consciousness, objective truth, and the power of reason. Beyond this general orientation, however, the comedy thriller in its specific subject matter offers an exploration of a central concern of the postmodern—the simultaneous awareness and playful deferral of death. Arthur Kroker, in his preface to *The Postmodern Scene* stresses, as do many theorists, a double vision of the postmodern. We are living, Kroker suggests "on the violent edge between ecstasy and decay," between a lament over "the death of the grand signifiers of modernity" such as consciousness and truth and the "ecstatic nihilism of ultramodernism," between "the body as a torture-chamber and pleasure-palace." It is within the body that Kroker locates the postmodern, with its "fateful oscillation" between the finality of "the body as death trap" and the seemingly infinite playful possibilities of the body as a Nietzschean "dancing star" in a universe of absence and darkness.[19] Kroker's employment of a term, death trap, that is also the title of one of the best-known of the comedy thrillers may serve as a reminder that these theatrical pieces are deeply implicated in subject as well as technique in these contemporary matters. In the game world of these plays—with their ghostly struggles of power—identities shift, deception reigns, truth dissolves, and the only certainty lies in the phenomenon that occupies the center of the action but also occupies the center of its web of confusion and misdirection— death itself. The games played by comedy thriller authors and their audiences have profound echoes, suggesting some of the deepest concerns and fears of contemporary culture.

2 THE SCENE OF THE CRIME

*". . . the only world you can inhabit is a dead world
—a country house world where peers and colonels
die in their studies."*

—**Milo Tindle in** *Sleuth*

Students, fans, and authors of modern detective fiction have long recognized that this popular field of writing has developed a number of fairly distinct subgenres, although these are given a variety of names. Each subgenre has its own, often quite distinct, type of detective, method of procedure, type of character, setting, style, mood, and language. Doubtless the most widely recognized subgenres are the American "hard-boiled" private-eye narratives, whose narrative generally follows a kind of quest structure, and the British domestic "cozies," whose narrative is traditionally the sifting of evidence involving a closed circle of suspects to determine "whodunnit." In Anthony Berkeley's classic story *The Poisoned Chocolates Case* (1929) one of the characters, echoing, probably unconsciously, a common distinction in modern German literary theory,[1] suggests that these two types of mysteries might be designated as "closed" or "open." "By a closed murder I mean one committed in a certain closed circle of persons, such as a house-party, in which it is known that the murderer is limited to membership of that actual group. This is by far the commoner form in fiction. An open murder I call one in which the criminal is not limited to any particular group but might be almost any one in the whole world. This, of course, is almost invariably what happens in real life."[2]

It will be immediately clear that in addition to being "open" and "closed" in terms of the possible suspects, these genres are also distinctly "open" and "closed" in terms of physical setting. The prototype of the closed setting is the British country house, since this type of mystery is, typically, as confined socially as it is geographically. George Grella observes that "the novel invariably presents murder in isolated and luxurious surroundings," a setting that "limits the suspects to a manageable number and establishes an aura of wealth and gentility."[3] While American private eye fictions return to the physical location of the classic works of Poe and Doyle—the complex, unbounded web of the modern city's streets—the English, as David Lehman points out, are much better at the "masterpiece-theatre" country house murder, "for the simple reason that English fiction can easily tap into a familiar past, a recognizable class structure, a code of manners, and a terrain of short distances and definite places, while the governing condition of most American fiction is a sense of continual transition, expanding frontiers, social fluidity and short-term trends."[4] Although both subgenres are well represented in film and on stage, the traditional narrative structure and the comparative flexibility of represented space make it clear that film is much better suited for the representation of the world of the hard-boiled detective story (indeed, this is the major source for the whole *film noir* tradition). The stage performance, particularly the modern realistic theatre, with its preference for single interiors, its circumscribed cast of characters, and its sense of entrapment, is much better suited for the presentation of the contrasting world of the "cozy." Nor should the observation of the Berkeley character that the former is more like "real life" be forgotten, for, as we shall see, this observation has important performative implications that go considerably beyond the obvious point that the camera can, technically, take us more easily into "real" settings than can the stage.

In a later chapter I will consider a few contemporary stage examples of the private eye form, but despite the continuing popularity of this style in the novel and in films, the much more typical stage detective narrative still follows the traditional patterns of the British "cozy." The type is well illustrated by Christie's apparently eternal *Mousetrap* and engagingly parodied by Stoppard in *The Real Inspector Hound*. The setting for such works is most commonly a well-to-do British country home, preferably one, as Lehman notes, isolated by both geography and inclement weather to intensify the aura of entrapment. The Muldoon Manor of Tom Stoppard's parody epitomizes such venues, not only in its Queen Anne elegance, but in its isolation, remarked upon by the help, Mrs. Drudge:

> Many visitors have remarked on the topographical quirk in the local strata whereby there are no roads leading from the Manor, though there *are* ways of getting *to* it, weather allowing.[5]

In this isolated world are gathered a collection of people, often with mysterious and unconfirmable backgrounds, one of whom is a murderer and one an official or unofficial detective. One or more murders are committed, suspicion is directed against a variety of the characters, and at last the true murderer—ideally a character who will both surprise the audience and yet, when the clues are properly assembled and explained, seem the inevitable choice—is revealed.

The tradition of the modern comedy thriller, from *Sleuth* to *Accomplice*, draws heavily upon the tradition of the cozy, but there are also significant yet sufficiently predictable differences, so that we may speak of a new sub-genre, with its own set of working codes. The closest and most obvious tie to the traditional cozy is the setting. When the curtain opens in either type of play, the setting is almost invariably a complex and moneyed interior, most likely a large gathering room like a garden room or hall on a country estate. Thus Agatha Christie's *The Mousetrap* is set in the Great Hall at Monkswell Manor and *Towards Zero* (1956) in the drawing-room at Gull's Point, Lady Tressilian's house at Saltcreek, Cornwall, "a large, very beautiful room, obviously belonging to somebody with exquisite taste."[6] Similarly, Anthony Shaffer's *Sleuth* takes place in the stone-flagged living room of Andrew Wyke's Norman Manor House in Wiltshire, and Rupert Holmes's *Accomplice* is set in the living room of Dorping Mill, "the renovated moorland residence of Derek and Janet Taylor . . . a paean to what level of affluence the English upper class can, in the 1970s, reasonably aspire."[7]

If there is any immediately observable difference between the "typical" setting of a modern comedy thriller and that of a more traditional detective play, it is surely in the geographical location of the setting. Though both are likely to depict large and elegantly furnished living rooms in the homes of the monied classes, the normal site of such homes has moved from the country to the city, the Park Avenue apartment has replaced the stately country home. Thus Eric Elice and Roger Rees's *Double Double* (1986) takes place in the "elegantly and expensively furnished" James's apartment in Connaught Square, London.[8] The same rule is followed when this type of play is set in America, so that we find Bob Barry's *Murder among Friends* (1976) set in an "opulent and beautifully decorated . . . duplex apartment in the Grammercy (sic) Park section of New York City";[9] Walter and Peter Marks's *The Butler Did It* set in an "opulent" Art Deco living room of a New York apartment where "a large window Upstage Center reveals the glittering skyline and a blue cyclorama";[10] and Richard Levinson and William Link's *Guilty Conscience* (1985) set in the "expensively-furnished" living room of the Jamison townhouse "in the east 60's."[11]

Since the implied social milieu has seemingly not radically changed, this shift from rural to urban domiciles may seem nothing more than an attempt to give this rather old-fashioned genre a more up-to-date appearance, but in terms of genre codification, far more fundamental issues are in fact involved. We have already noted the traditional and close relationship between the "closed" world of the country house mystery and the "open" one of the city streets. By moving their settings to city apartments, these recent authors automatically place them in a more "open" context, in a world distinctly less predictable than the established routine of the self-contained country mansion.

This geographical departure from a milieu associated with predictability and closure is totally in keeping with the new world of instability characteristic of the comedy thriller. Many theorists have seen the traditional detective story as a kind of moral fable in which a happy and orderly world is temporarily disrupted by the act of murder and restored to equilibrium by the detective's discovery, and hence purging, of the destabilizing murderer. One of the best-known statements of this interpretation was "The Guilty Vicarage," by W. H. Auden. Here Auden discusses the role of the story's setting, suggesting that it should be "Eden-like," because this emphasizes the upsetting and out-of-place quality of the murder. "The country is preferable to the town," he continues, "a well-to-do neighborhood (but not too well-to-do—or there will be a suspicion of ill-gotten gains) better than a slum."[12] This milieu accords well with Auden's interpretation of such fictions as parables of an innocent world falling from grace by a murder and being redeemed by a savior detective, but it is clear that the favored milieu of these modern comedy thrillers (like that of the hard-boiled detective stories) is much more morally ambiguous. The physical surroundings suggest no rural Eden but an all-too-sophisticated urban background, inhabited by characters who on the whole would be little disturbed by Auden's "suspicion of ill-gotten gains."

Nevertheless, a detailed realistic interior suggesting an elegant upper class existence, whether urban or rural, is likely to seem a familiar world to either the reader of the opening stage directions in a comedy thriller or to the audience member at the rise of the curtain, since this is essentially the traditional world of the mystery novel or detective play. In fact, as we shall see, this impression is often calculatedly deceptive. Since the physical setting of the traditional cozy is as highly codified as any other element in the genre, we should not be surprised to find that it is subject to the same parodic subversion in the comedy thriller. Richard Levinson and William Link's *Guilty Conscience* is set in the living room of the Jamison townhouse in the East 60s, one of New York's most expensive neighborhoods, but the stage directions open on an odd note: "the set, as we shall discover, is something of a chameleon, but for the moment we are only aware of an expensively-furnished room and its accouterments."[13]

Rarely are the opening stage directions so revealing as this (and of course an audience in the theatre would not, in any case, have this information), but the "chameleon" setting is widely found in modern comedy thrillers and contributes very importantly to the particular self-consciousness and instability of their fictive worlds. The real radicalism of these settings is never observable when the curtain opens—indeed an important part of the operation of such settings is that they should be assumed to be no different from the settings of the familiar literary and dramatic traditions of mystery fiction.

If, as Berkeley's character observed, the closed world of the cozy is already more removed from "real life" than the open world of the hard-boiled procedural, then the comedy thriller is a step further removed, heading toward a world of pure fictionality based upon the manipulation of fictive tropes and devices. The very predictability and conventionality of the traditionally detailed interior setting allow it to function not only as a quick orienting device for an audience who is familiar with the codes of the genre, but also as a convenient means for destabilizing those codes as soon as its predictability and conventionality are foregrounded. The opening stage description of *Out of Sight*—

Out of Murder (1983) illustrates this potential perfectly: "the action of the play takes place in the living room of a very old mansion in Vermont. Not a typical Vermont house, the room looks more like the setting for a Victorian mystery."[14]

Even the most "realistic" of the comedy thriller settings tend to have a touch of the theatrical or the ludic about them, and some become, frankly, "settings." Anthony Shaffer's *Whodunnit* begins with a speech delivered to the audience in darkness by the murderer that informs them, in part "what you have stumbled into tonight is nothing more or less than an old-fashioned closed circle, telephone wires have been cut, flood-waters have washed away the bridge, 'My God you mean it has to be one of us' English country house whodunnit."[15] Atmospheric effects often supplement this self-conscious quotation of a theatrical tradition. Thunder and lightning punctuate ominous moments in the action and often help "set the stage" as in *Murder among Friends,* which begins "The curtain rises on a dark stage. A moment. Thunder and lightning. The flash of lightning briefly illuminates the set,"[16] or as in Anthony Shaffer's *Whodunnit,* where, after an opening speech given in darkness by the murderer, "the curtain rises slowly and there is a crash of thunder and lightning." The use of this device near the end of the first act of Bernard Slade's *Fatal Attraction* (1986) self-consciously situates us both in the tradition and in the structure of this particular text:

> GUS: In police work I've found that the obvious usually turns out to be true. Also the hero or heroine gets killed at the end of Act One. (There is a clap of thunder outside and rain starts to come down.)[17]

In a number of thrillers, the furnishings of the displayed room also are clearly to be taken as theatricalized indices to the action to be performed here. The "game-playing" that characterizes *Sleuth* is echoed in the collections of combat games that fill the room and the rather manic world-view of its leading character in the full-sized mechanical "Laughing Sailor," whose grotesque "voice" will be the last heard in this play. The magic tricks and devices that fill the protagonist's apartment in John Pielmeier's *Sleight of Hand* provide a clear warning to the audience that this is a world of illusion and misdirection. The dual themes of theatre and murder are announced by the framed theatrical window cards and the guns, handcuffs, maces, broadswords, and battle-axes that decorate the walls of Sidney Bruhl's study in Ira Levin's *Deathtrap.* The possibilities of utilizing modern computer technology for thriller "games" was the basis, interestingly enough, of both of the new New York comedy thrillers appearing in the fall of 1992, Rupert Holmes's *Solitary Confinement* and George W. George and Jeff Travers's *Program for Murder.* The setting of the former is a lavish tower study, the abode of multimillionaire Richard Jannings, dominated by a huge video screen which is Jannings's only contact with the outside world. The screen and most of the room's furnishings are controlled by a large computer bank in one wall. After Jannings is murdered (or seems to be murdered), a program that automatically flows from this computer to the screen engages in a life or death series of games with the murderer, trapped in the room. The situation is very close to an electronic version of the mental duel between Bruhl and Anderson in *Deathtrap.*

Program for Murder is set in an elaborate Victorian living room in Cambridge, Massachusetts—a room in which the Victorian decor is almost obliterated by computer banks and snaking cables, the work of the current inhabitant. Jeremy, the protagonist, has made his reputation by inventing a complex video game, the "Monster Machine," an example of which occupies a prominent upstage position. Here, as in *Solitary Confinement,* the computer enters into the game of life and death, with the added possibility, in *Program for Murder,* that Alexis, the master computer, may have become a character with its own agenda, like the notorious Hal in the film *2001.*

Such settings and effects are derived, of course, from a long tradition of popular entertainment, stretching back through the Victorian mysteries to the gothic melodramas, and it is partly under the influence of this tradition that the comfortably well-to-do country houses Auden associates with the traditional detective story become the more ominous, threatening, and unstable halls of mystery often found in the comedy thriller. In the Gothic drama too, the settings were much more likely to be the domain of intriguing aristocracy than Edenic innocence. Such settings echoed the duplicity of their inhabitants with architectural duplicity—trap doors, secret passageways, trick mirrors, all manner of strange and hidden machinery. The crumbling ancestral castle of the Gothic drama may seem far removed from the elegant modern urban flat, but its ominous architectural secrets remain, as may be seen in the stage directions for the second scene of Gerald Moon's *Corpse!*:

> A gilt dophin at the bottom of the banister rail turns on a pivot and is a secret control knob to open double doors hidden in the downstage right pillar. This reveals a huge walk-in drinks cabinet with shelves of glasses and bottles. This should be built so that an actor can be shut up inside, having been impaled against the shelves with a trick sword.[18]

Trap doors in floors and ceiling have long been essential for the shocking and frequently grisly surprises of the gothic tradition, and the authors of comedy thrillers have found them still extremely useful, even in the most contemporary circumstances. The police sergeant in *An Act of the Imagination* (1988) sets a trap for the murderer which involves installing in the wall of the suspect's home a traditional theatrical reversible panel, plain on one side and with blood and brains on the other, so as to fake a shooting death. He sees this as a theatrical device, remarking that the presumed victim is not only a good actress but is also experienced in the use of such "special effects."[19] Central to the action of *Fatal Attraction*, set in a modern Nantucket beach house, is a living room jacuzzi, whose relationship to the hidden

alcove of the Gothic drama is clearly suggested by its introduction:

> BLAIR glances out of the window once more, moves to bookcase,
> removes about three books, and pushes a concealed button. A
> five by three square of the floor D.L. slides open revealing a
> jacuzzi. It is important that when it is closed the grooved wooden
> floor completely disguises it.[20]

Both the living and the dead are hidden in this jacuzzi as the
play progresses. A striking example of its usage occurs at the
end of the first act, soon after the reflexive line by Gus about
first act murders. The threatened heroine Blair, left alone on
stage, turns out the lamps and places on the stereo a recording
of Bartok's "Concerto for Orchestra," described in the stage directions as "quiet at first, faintly ominous." She then bolts the
front door, takes coffee things to the adjoining kitchen, and
turns out the lights there. She is about to press the button opening the jacuzzi when a wicker pot on an overhead beam crashes
down, just missing her. Shaken, she picks up the plant, then
presses the jacuzzi controls. As she moves away, undoing her
robe and looking at the beam, the jacuzzi top slides open and
Tony Lombardi, a photojournalist who has been haunting her,
leaps out, soaking wet and brandishing a knife. Blair, her robe
undone, turns to face him and they stand motionless for a long
moment.[21] This pantomime sequence and tableau draws together many of the traditional elements of the gothic thriller—
mysterious and ominous events surrounding an endangered
heroine, the sudden and shocking appearance of a fearful figure
from a place of concealment, the threat of both sexual abuse
and murder, even a proper musical background.

Much more abrupt and shocking, more in the style of the
grand guignol than the gothic thriller, is the trap door device
that ends the first act of Simon Gray's *Stage Struck* (1979). The
setting is a modernized farmhouse, the home of Anne, a successful actress, and her husband Robert, a failed actor, stage

manager, and playwright. At the climax of a confrontation between Robert and Anne's psychoanalyst, the psychoanalyst asks
"She's either left you or leaving you, isn't she?" to which Robert
replies, "No, she's not. You can see her for yourself. In fact, she's
coming straight down to give you her greetings and her thanks."
Here he pulls on the rope that opens the trap door, calling out
"Darling—you're on!" The bound and hanged body of Anne
plummets down, tongue protruding, eyes bulging, a knife
plunged in its chest. The lights black out and the curtain falls
to Robert's insane laughter.[22]

So sudden and horrifying is this effect that the audience is
unlikely to recall until later how grotesquely theatrical it also is,
with the dead actress making her "entrance" at the command
of her husband/stage manager. The opening of the next act,
however, foregrounds this theatricalization as, a few seconds
later, the husband and doctor are discovered standing by the
"body" discussing its effectiveness. We find that it is in fact a
dummy, an effect used previously in the theatre by Robert and
set up by him here in an (unsuccessful) attempt to terrify the
doctor.

A far more elaborate, and more disturbing, version of this
same device is utilized in the ingenious opening of Anthony
Shaffer's *Murderer* (1979), a thirty-minute pantomime during
which we witness the apparent murder and graphic dismemberment of a model by a painter. Just as the crime is completed
and the blood cleaned up, a suspicious police sergeant arrives.
Poking about the room, he at last opens the stove, and pulls out
the partially burned head and a leg. Only then do we find that
the ghastly dismemberment we have just witnessed was not
performed on a living character but on a dummy. The painter's
excuse is that he enjoys the reenactment of famous crimes, but
in fact he knows that a prying neighbor is watching him through
a picture window and has called the police. All of this, he subsequently reveals to the unharmed model, is part of an elaborate
plot which will allow him to commit a real murder "without

attracting the least suspicion or interference. The police would just think it was one of my games."[23]

I will return later to the significance of the false death itself in the epistemological world of the comedy thriller, but presently I would like to focus not on the false death itself, but on the peculiarly theatrical manner of its presentation. In both of these cases (and in many others in the genre), the death is consciously "staged" by the protagonist to frighten or to mislead another character. In both cases, of course, the real intended victim of the illusion is the actual theatre audience, who is being manipulated by the dramatist in precisely the same manner as his character seeks to manipulate his stage victim. The neighbor observing the dismemberment through the picture window is a mirror image of ourselves, watching the same scene through the proscenium arch. Likewise, the doctor stands in for us as the trap door reveals its horrible and totally unexpected secret. And far from muting this parallel between our reactions and those of the "audience" in the dramatic world, these plays call the parallel to our attention by the specific use of the language of theatre and of enactment ("Darling—you're on!" "You mean you've been play-acting you were him?"). In Ira Levin's *Deathtrap*, one of the most complex and self-reflexive works in this genre, this process is specifically discussed in the second act, where Clifford points out to Sidney why the murder plot they carried out together in the previous act would make an effective theatrical piece:

> Try to see it all from an audience's viewpoint. *Everything we did to convince Myra that she was seeing a real murder—would have exactly the same effect on them.* Weren't *we* giving a play? Wasn't *she* our audience? Scene One: Julien tells Doris about this terrific play that's come in the mail. He jokes about killing for it, then calls Willard and invites him over, getting him to bring the original copy. Audience thinks exactly what Doris thinks. Julien might kill Willard. Scene Two. *Everything that happened from the moment we came through that door.* All the little ups and downs we put in to make it ring true: the I'm-expecting-a-phone-call

bit, everything. Tightened up a little, naturally. And then the strangling, which scares the audience as much as it does Doris.[24]

Although what we are seeing is still being presented in the fictive "real world" of the play, the theatrical and performative qualities of the action—a fiction rehearsed and presented by certain of the characters for another as "audience"—are foregrounded. Indeed if Clifford's hopes were realized and his play actually presented, what would be seen would be essentially no different from what has just occurred in the play's "real world." Such is the result of calling attention to the performative function of this sort of murder plot.

Much is made, and rightly so, of the relationship between magic and murder on stage in John Pielmeier's *Sleight of Hand*. The first act is set in a magician's apartment, full of murderous illusions and hidden passageways, and the second act takes place on the darkened stage of a similar house of illusions, the theatre. There is a more or less self-consciously theatricalized quality in all thrillers, and in all thriller settings, haunted as they necessarily are not with the ghosts of real-life experiences but with the workings of a literary and dramatic genre—one, moreover, particularly associated with illusion and misdirection. The utilization of an onstage "audience" foregrounds even more distinctly this sense that what we see on stage is not in fact a room in a baronial hall or an elegant urban apartment, but rather a kind of stage set.

In such thrillers as *Murderer, Sleight of Hand, Deathtrap*, or *Stage Struck*, this theatricalization of the stage world remains essentially metaphorical. Although the painter "stages" his murder for the "audience" neighbor, we are still expected to accept his studio as a "real" studio, though converted into a kind of stage. We thus remain in the realm of traditional dramatic illusion, though rather tenuously, since the characters' own theatricalization of their actions serves as a challenge to and partial erosion of that illusion. The detailed physical surroundings offered to us by these plays and the traditions of the genre encourage us to accept the fictive "reality" of the setting, while the apparent generic self-consciousness displayed by both actors and physical surroundings simultaneously subverts this acceptance.

The tension operating here is similar to and perhaps even more extreme than that noted by Jonathan Culler in his discussion of the poetics of the novel. According to Culler, the basic convention which governs the novel is that it will produce a world,[25] a convention surely equally basic to the theatre, which offers an ostended world of even more tangible reality. Deviations from the coherence of this established world, Culler argues, are "more troubling and therefore potentially more powerful" in the novel than in poetry, where they can be more easily recuperated as "moments of visionary or prophetic stance." Nevertheless, even when the novel is not engaged (as it may be in modern experiments) in undermining our notions of coherence and significance, its creative use of these notions causes "that which is taken as natural" to be "brought to consciousness and revealed as process, as construct."[26]

Surely our awareness of the creative operations of theatre results in a similar undermining, particularly when the operations are so strongly foregrounded as they are in the comedy thrillers. Simultaneously with the creation of their fictive worlds the constant use of traditional generic settings, characters, properties, situations, and even sound effects, provides an ongoing reminder of the artificiality, the "constructedness" of this world, not infrequently underlined, as in the plays just mentioned, by frequent visual and spoken reference to the world of the theatre and the theatricality of the play's world.

This dynamic, as I have noted, occurs even when the thriller remains, as most thrillers do, within the realm of conventional dramatic illusion. But the employment of self-reflexive elements has become so widespread in this genre, and thereby the audience awareness of the "theatricalization" of this material so common, that it is hardly surprising that among the more recent

examples of the genre may be found some in which the setting
is no longer regarded metaphorically as a stage by its fictive
inhabitants, but actually is recognized as a stage setting by
them. I am not here thinking of a setting like that of the second
act of *Sleight of Hand,* which announces itself in the program as
set on the stage of a darkened theatre, and which iconically
represents itself as a stage from the rise of the curtain. Such a
setting naturally foregrounds the theatricalism of the action but
is not essentially different in its reception by the audience from
more conventional "realistic" salons and living rooms.

A far more radical, and more subversive, use of the stage
occurs when the thriller begins in what appears to be (and may
even be identified in the program as) a conventional salon or
living room and is accepted as such by the audience and (apparently) by the characters until, at some point in the action, it is
revealed that what we have been watching is not the true
"world" of this play, but a staged rehearsal. One might consider
this as the equivalent for the physical surroundings of the device
already widely used for at least some of the thriller characters—
the presumed "victim" that turns out to be an illusion, a theatrical dummy. Here we find a presumed "room" that turns out to
be also an illusion, a theatrical substitution. The effect on the
audience, as with the dummy, is one of disorientation, but on a
far more fundamental level, since now the entire epistemological
basis of the action must shift.

The Butler Did It provides an excellent example of this device,
both in execution and preparation. The reader will have noted
that the titles of comedy thrillers normally attempt to suggest
their genre. Many simply ring variations on *Murder,* though
Deathtrap, Stage Struck, and *Sleight of Hand* cleverly suggest the
manipulation of dramatic illusion that has become so central to
this genre. *Whodunnit* and *The Butler Did It,* both strong examples of the increasing self-reflexivity of this genre, signal this
fact in their titles, foregrounding not only generic expectations,
but in the latter case, even a reference to the most overused and

banal of such expectations. From such a title, a potential audience member might reasonably expect a strong measure of parodic self-consciousness, an expectation that would surely be confirmed by a reading of the program before the performance, since the program reveals that the characters of the play are Raymond Butler, Angela Butler, Victoria Butler, and their butler, Aldo, as well as Detective Mumford and one Anthony J. Lefcourt.

This parodic flavor certainly carries into the first scene, set in an elegant New York apartment at Christmastime and played, according to the stage directions "in an arch, stylized manner." Scarcely has the scene begun with a brief family spat, than Mrs. Butler clutches her throat and dies. Aldo, somewhat inexplicably, suggests that the body be hidden in the window seat, advice which the others, equally inexplicably, immediately follow. As they stand or sit about the room attempting to sort out their emotions, we are startled to see the "dead" Mrs. Butler appearing *behind* the window seat, apparently outside the window, and creeping offstage left. No sooner has Mrs. Butler made her strange reappearance than Anthony J. Lefcourt runs up onto the stage, from the audience side of the proscenium, by means of a set of stairs on the side aisle, stopping what is now revealed as a rehearsal of a play he has written and is directing. The window seat is now seen to be merely a part of the back wall of a setting, and "Mrs. Butler's" reappearance nothing more remarkable than an actress leaving the stage. The remainder of the action, though it contains many surprises and some passages of extremely revealing self-analysis to which I will return later, provides no further epistemological jolts of this extremity, but the basic convention of the secure fictive world has been shattered, and the way has been prepared for even more radical subversions of this world, such as we will find in Rupert Holmes's *Accomplice,* which is designed primarily to subvert the audience's attempts to apply normal readings to it.

If, as Geoffrey Hartman has suggested, "to solve a crime in

detective stories means to give it an exact location, to pinpoint not merely the murderer and his motives, but also the very place, the room, the ingenious or brutal circumstances,"[27] then the increasing inclination of comedy thrillers to undermine the authenticity of this place, first by emphasizing its theatrical and illusory nature and, ultimately, to deny its very reality, involves, in this changing attitude toward the setting, a refusal to allow solution of the crime and, thus, a specific rejection of the end-oriented pleasure. The types of characters placed in the comedy thriller world and the types of actions they pursue are also, as we shall see, developed in opposition to the normal expectations of mystery fiction, but the settings themselves, solid and traditional as they normally appear as the curtain rises, ultimately are revealed as constructs as free from stabilizing authority as any element in the illusive world of postmodern discourse.

3 AMONG THOSE PRESENT

"You've got to have at least ten highly unlikely people for the audience to choose from—and they're the ones that get my goat—the suspects."
—Penny in *Amber for Anna*

The physical world of the modern comedy thriller does not appear, at least upon first inspection, to be markedly different from that of the traditional detective drama, even though, as we have seen, this initial impression may be quite erroneous. When we turn from the setting to the characters of these more recent works, however, we find that, as a rule, the cast of characters has markedly changed and, moreover, changed in so consistent a way that it would not be exaggerating to speak of new character configurations that may be considered one of the distinguishing features of this genre.

The characters of the traditional cozy tend to be as predictable as the country house where they gather. George Grella argues both engagingly and convincingly that both setting and characters in this genre are derived from the conventions and types of the English comedy of manners. Aside from "the bourgeois detective and the tramp who is always initially suspect," the characters tend to form a microcosm of British upper-class society—the professional man, the vicar, the beef-witted squire, the comic pedant, the stuffy butler, and the young lovers who will be united at the end but in the meantime generally confuse matters through the young man's efforts to protect the girl "by destroying or manufacturing evidence, providing false alibis, and generally behaving like a gentleman." Like the comedy of manners, the detective novel removes from society the undesirable elements that prevent the happiness of those remaining. Thus the victim must be flawed in some way, socially or ethically, and though the murderer therefore performs a kind of service to society, he or she too must be flawed, "since 'good' (i.e. socially valuable) people cannot permanently suffer in comedy."[1]

This highly predictable group is often carried over from the traditional novel to the traditional detective play (and, like other aspects of such plays, is engagingly parodied in Stoppard's *The Real Inspector Hound*), but such a configuration is in fact remarkably rare in the comedy thrillers of the 1970s and 1980s. Indeed, only three such plays, less than one in ten, offers such a case. Significantly, in each of these cases the device is used with obvious self-consciousness and the "characters" are ultimately revealed not as "real" persons in the fictive world but as fictional constructs, though their use is quite different in each play.

In Fred Carmichael's *Out of Sight—Out of Murder* a mystery author who has created a group of characters but lacks inspiration for a story seeks to find it by moving to a gloomy Victorian house in Vermont where another author has died. As he works, the characters appear—all standard types from traditional mysteries—full of suggestions about how they might be used. To fans of mystery drama, this situation will very likely recall one of the great American classics of the genre, George M. Cohan's *Seven Keys to Baldpate* (1913), whose bizarre and surprising plot in fact comes closer than any other early twentieth-century mystery play to anticipating certain concerns and strategies of the modern comedy thriller. In Cohan's play, as in Carmichael's, a writer spends a night in a "haunted" locale, in this case on a bet that he cannot write a novel in such surroundings. A variety of characters like those of traditional fiction show up and fill his night with confusion and incident, at the end of which two surprising revelations are made. The first is that these "characters" were really actors hired by the owner of the house to interfere with the author and with the bet, and the second is that all of this, even the first revelation, is in fact the plot of the book that the author has successfully written during this evening. The situation of *Out of Sight* also inevitably recalls Pirandello's *Six Characters in Search of an Author*, even to the writer in the former who remarks, when the characters begin to appear, that "I'm like Pirandello. I've got six characters in search of me," to which his first "character," the sophisticated and doomed Lydia, replies "Pirandello's a bore. I worked for him once."[2]

Walter and Peter Marks's *The Butler Did It* and Anthony Shaffer's *Whodunnit*, the other two comedy thrillers with fairly traditional casts of characters, suggest, even by their titles, that these character selections are to be taken as conscious "quotations" from a familiar tradition, as markers in a literary game with its conventions foregrounded. As has already been noted, audiences of *The Butler Did It* are alerted to the parodic quality of this play, even before the curtain rises, not only by the title, but by the information in the program that every member of the cast, except the detective and one outsider, is either a member of the Butler family or a real butler. A few minutes into the play this onomastic self-consciousness is extended to the entire fictive world as a "director" bounds onto the stage, like Hinkfuss in Pirandello's *Tonight We Improvise* (1930), and we find that what we have been watching is a rehearsal of "The Butler Did It," a play written by this director and characterized by him as a "classic whodunnit."[3]

Whodunnit also employs a Pirandellian consciousness of itself as a theatrical artifice, but instead of abruptly puncturing the fictive world, as in *The Butler Did It*, *Whodunnit* gradually erodes it by a series of generically self-conscious observations by different characters. The opening speech, which reveals that we are about to witness "an old-fashioned closed circle . . . 'My God you mean it has to be one of us' English country house whodunnit," signals by its jocular tone a parodic consciousness, but since it is delivered in the dark before the action begins, it can be taken as a sort of separate prologue and, thus, less illusion-challenging than a similar comment within the play might be. As the characters are introduced during the first act, the sense of parody remains strongly marked in both situation and dialogue. The oily Levantine Capodistriou, clearly marked for the victim, confides in Perkins, the butler, almost at once in this self-conscious dialogue:

> PERKINS: What's your game?
> CAPODISTRIOU: Blackmail.
> PERKINS: Blackmail?
> CAPODISTRIOU: Precisely. As in the phrase, "Blackmail—that's an ugly word, Inspector."[4]

Indeed, Capodistriou greets each new house guest with knowledge of some dark and bizarre secret in their past and the threat of its revelation. His decapitation by an unseen murderer ends the first act.

The Inspector, arriving, as is customary, in the second act to investigate the murder, begins the traditional interrogation of the suspects with an observation that provides a striking "fictionalization" of both characters and situation:

> INSPECTOR: . . . it seems to me, that I may have been fortunate towards the end of a longish career in run of the mill villainy, to find myself for the first time investigating what I believe is called a classic, closed circle, English country house murder, with half a dozen archetypical suspects such as you would find in books, and a butler. So don't lets spoil it by routine protests. (He looks significantly at DASHWELL)
> DASHWELL: What are you looking at me for? I don't know anything about this. I haven't done anything. I'm innocent, do you hear me. Absolutely innocent.

INSPECTOR: That sort of protest is perfectly permissible, as long
as it's done in character. You, Rear Admiral, can bluster but
not whine. You, Lady Tremurrain, can voice your innocence
in terms of haughty aphorism. You young people can be racily
disrespectful of the might of the law, whilst you, Mr. Bazeby,
and you, Dame Edith, can be respectively fustian and frump-
ish. As for you, Perkins, your role is to grovel polysyllabically.
PERKINS: I don't know what you're on about.[5]

To the clear consternation of the suspects, the Inspector insists upon basing his investigation of the crime entirely upon
traditional generic expectations. He refuses even to call in the
maid and the cook since they "wouldn't rate" in country house
murders where the prime suspects must be precisely those characters that now surround him: "Rear Admirals, dotty female
archaeologists, grand titled ladies, demure debs, stuffy lawyers,
and rapscallion nephews newly returned from Australia," not
to mention that "most favorite suspect of all," the butler, though
the Inspector confesses that he personally "cannot recall a single
detective story in which the butler actually did do it."

The Rear Admiral begins to protest all this "blithering tom-
foolery" about "country house murders and archetypical suspects," but as he does so, a strange thing happens. According
to the stage directions: "While he has been talking his mous-
tache has fallen off. Very elaborately and highly embarrassed,
he tries to put it back on again but fails. The others look aghast.
The audience must think it's a mistake." At this point, well into
the second act, the play finally exposes the trap that has been
both set and hinted at from the beginning: these prototypical
"characters" are in fact fictions played by actors, each of them
a specialist in that particular "type." The "Rear Admiral," for
example, removes his wig and beard and announces that his
"real name" is "Jeremy Fielder, well known on screen and stage
for endearing portrayals of crusty colonels, cantankerous cler-
ics, and surly seafarers."[6] One particularly striking touch occurs
when the actor who was playing the "rapscallion nephew," in

noting his specialties and stage credits, lists, among his recent roles, Milo Tindle in Shaffer's earlier comedy thriller, the well-known *Sleuth,* a reference particularly apt since Milo's appearance in disguise was one of the major tricks in that play.

Each of these dramas develops its foregrounding of the theatrical in quite a different way. In *Out of Sight,* there is no murder at all in the play's "real" world. The murder and most of the action in fact take place in the fictive world of the characters, which is temporarily entered by their author. *The Butler Did It* and *Whodunnit* both begin in a fictive world not fully recognized as such by the audience; in the first, this is the rehearsal of a detective drama, in the second, a kind of "mystery weekend." After a murder occurs in each, we shift to the "real world," with the characters of the previous situation now revealed as actors. In *The Butler Did It,* the "murder" remains in the fictive world, though another "false" murder and a real one still lie ahead in this "real" world. In *Whodunnit,* the murder is "real" in both worlds. Thus the "worlds" of these three plays, and the way their participants relate to them, are very different. What is consistent, however, is that in every case, the traditional characters of detective fiction are presented as constructs, as fictional "roles" or "types," opposed in each case by a "reality," presumably closer to our own. Thus, only in this "quoted" manner, like Pirandellian characters, do the familiar fictional types of the classic detective story enter the reflexive world of the comedy thriller.

The highly self-conscious theatricalization of the conventional country house mystery has become so common that a new work in the Christie tradition, even if it is not, strictly speaking, a comedy thriller, may feel it necessary to acknowledge the contemporary audience's consciousness of the artifice in this genre. In many respects, John Glines's *Murder in Disguise* (1992) looks back to plays like Christie's *Mousetrap,* with the isolated wealthy country house setting and the cast of characters with mysterious backgrounds—one of them bent on revenging a childhood wrong—but it is also much more self-conscious, particularly in respect to character roles. Although this is a drama of gay relationships, *Murder in Disguise* is by no means a camp travesty of Christie. The conventions of the genre are taken seriously, even when (as in the impenetrable fog around the house and the cut telephone lines) they come perilously close to parody. On the other hand, while the play basically follows the traditional country house murder scenario, it continually foregrounds the process of role-playing. Here, as in *Whodunnit*, a "murder game" is played, with everyone taking an assumed role. During this, a real murder is committed. The actor designated as the "detective" cross-examines the "suspects," though, since these are only roles in the game, it is quite possible that he too may be the murderer. To add to the emphasis upon role instability, the "detective" asks that the other characters exchange masks and then questions each, not about his/her own past and motives, but about those of the other character whose mask he or she is now wearing. The murdered character is a twin (both parts played by the same actor), and the first act curtain, when the surviving twin appears in the murdered man's mask, is a moment that would be absolutely appropriate in the destablized world of identities of the comedy thriller. The murder is discovered near the end of the first act, and immediately afterward, the "brother" appears, wearing the murdered man's mask, to give the curtain line, "Why are you all looking at me?"

In fact, the standard modern comedy thriller has replaced the traditional grouping of suspects and detective of the country house murder with a configuration that is quite different but, by this time, almost as predictable in these plays as the odd assortment of British upper-class types in the classic cozies. First, we may note that the size of the cast is much reduced; most commonly there are only four or five actors and sometimes as few as three or even two. In *Deathtrap*, Sidney Bruhl, the successful writer of thrillers cynically, but not inaccurately, describes his activity as a disease: "thrilleritis malignis, the fevered pursuit of the one-set, five-character moneymaker."[7] The smaller cast in some measure reflects a general trend in the modern drama, but much more importantly, it reflects a new kind of story being told. Clearly, with a cast of two or even four, a dramatist cannot construct a situation involving a detective, a victim, and a reasonable number of suspects in the traditional manner. What this genre has done is shift from one highly conventionalized pattern to another which, in the theatre, has been equally conventionalized—the French triangle play of amorous intrigue. At the center of almost every thriller of the 1970s and 1980s is found a husband, wife, and male or female lover, with two of them plotting the death of the third. This shift has doubtless been facilitated by the fact that certain conventions of this genre are shared with those of the comedy of manners, whose close relationship to the traditional detective story Grella has noted.

In the triangle play, as in the comedy of manners, the characters involved have sufficient financial resources, leisure time, and wit to create a private world of intricate and elaborate intrigue and counter-intrigue. Comedy of manners intrigue, ever since the Restoration, has been closely involved with fortune hunting and sexual rivalry, carried on through verbal wit and repartee, and this subject matter accords very nicely with both the triangle play and the comedy thriller. It is simply a matter of raising the stakes of the game to life and death instead of, or in addition to, fortune and reputation. Selwyn and Imogen in *Murder by the Book* (1982) do not let even the knowledge that each is plotting to murder the other dampen their pleasure in each others' conversation and ability at intrigue:

> IMOGEN: But John said . . .
> SELWYN: I know he did. That was another mendacious embellishment—
> IMOGEN:—to lure me into a false sense of security—
> SELWYN:—by suggesting an alternative suspect—
> IMOGEN:—WITH A PLAUSIBLE MOTIVE.

SELWYN: You know it's such fun to talk with someone who can truly appreciate my Machiavellian ways. You really are pure Borgia.
IMOGEN: Thank you.[8]

Grella points out that even the traditional detective story, as a further stylization of an already highly stylized form, "frequently exhibits a conscious tampering with conventions and becomes sophisticated self-parody."[9] This is even more obviously true of the comedy thriller, which draws not only upon the stylized world of the comedy of manners but also upon that of the triangle drama, behind which lie the carefully composed actions of the French well-made play. The tendency toward "sophisticated self-parody" in triangle drama can be seen as early as the end of the nineteenth century. The famous opening scene of Becque's *La Parisienne* (1885) employs a coup de théâtre that would not be at all out of place in a modern comedy thriller. The curtain rises on a fashionable drawing room. Clotilde, dressed to go out, enters hurriedly and conceals a letter underneath a writing case. As Lafont enters, she pretends to lock a small secretary desk, inspiring his opening line, "Open the desk and give me that letter." Clotilde refuses, and a tense scene ensues, during which Lafont expresses his suspicions of her infidelity while Clotilde berates him for his lack of trust in her. At last Lafont, driven almost to desperation, pleads:

> Think of me, Clotilde, and think of yourself. Reflect that a mistake is easily made and can never be mended. Don't give in to that taste for adventures which makes so many victims nowadays. Resist it, Clotilde, resist it. As long as you stay faithful to me, you remain worthy and respectable. If you should deceive me . . .

At this point Clotilde abruptly cuts him off and moves to the center door, exclaiming "Careful. Here comes my husband!"[10]

The effect of this scene is still stunning; it is based, of course, on the audience's full awareness that they are seeing the opening of a triangle play, encouraging them to employ the standard "reading" for that genre and interpret this scene as a quarrel between husband and wife, background for the amorous intrigue that will surely be developed later, and then disorienting them by revealing that they are witnessing a quite different angle on this familiar situation, a quarrel between the lovers at a later point in the liaison. The more familiar the audience is with the conventions, the greater the shock when they discover that these conventions were neither so transparent nor so reliable as they had assumed.

One of the most common plot devices of the comedy thriller is precisely this sort of surprise. A relationship of a particular character that we have been encouraged to "place" in the genre structure in some familiar way is suddenly revealed to be in fact fulfilling a quite different function or role. A complex, but typical, example occurs in Bob Barry's *Murder among Friends*. The scene opens with Ted and Angela naked beneath a fur rug in front of an apartment fire. She awakens from a nightmare and insists that they "call off" something. Ted refuses. Angela persists:

> ANGELA: Ted, please, I'll do anything for you, anything . . . but I can't . . . *(The words die in her throat)*
> TED: Don't be afraid to say it.
> ANGELA: I can't commit murder. I'm too civilized, and too rich.
> TED: The rich get away with murder. Besides, I'm pulling the trigger, not you.
> ANGELA: Ted, you're not on drugs, are you?
> TED: We've got to kill him.
> ANGELA: Wouldn't divorce be simpler?[11]

Though there is a faint hint here of the *Parisienne* turn, it is not likely that a modern audience, despite the intimate setting, will be extremely surprised at this point to discover that this is not a husband and wife but a wife and lover, and then we move quickly into familiar comedy thriller terrain. Much of the rest of the act is spent in going over the rather elaborate murder plot, which involves a paid killer and a faked robbery. Once this plot is laid out, the scene ends.

The second scene begins with a dialogue between Ted and the husband, Palmer. This time it is Ted who is expressing misgivings and Palmer who is strengthening his resolve to go through with the fake robbery and the murder, but now it is Angela who is the supposed victim, killed for her money by a new pair of lovers—Ted and Palmer. The shock of this new perspective, as in Becque's drama, demands a complete shifting of the interpretive strategy previously encouraged by the play, but in a much more radical way. In Becque, the surprising shift in the audience's interpretation of the scheme doubtless momentarily results in a foregrounding of the generic expectations that had set them up for the trick, but once the trick has been played, the drama settles back down again into a conventional, and largely predictable, pattern of action. No such immediate release is offered in *Murder among Friends*. Not only does the new scene deconstruct our reading of the earlier one, but the experience of the two scenes then continues to prevent the audience from taking either as representing "truth," since it is not clear which of the two "roles" Ted is playing is the truthful one. Both of his lovers are potential murderers, both potential victims, and Ted, in parallel scenes, has agreed to both contradictory plots. Generic expectations have been exposed not merely as arbitrary and potentially misleading, as in Becque, but as actively subversive of the coherent overarching pattern of action the genre of detective fiction traditionally has employed.

If there is anything predictable about the world of the comedy thriller, it is that every attempt will be made to mislead, frustrate, and surprise the expectations of the audience. In *Murder among Friends*, faced with two mutually exclusive plots set up in the first two scenes, the audience's expectation naturally turns to the upcoming scene where the plots will converge—the faked robbery. Will Ted kill Palmer with Angela's assistance, or will Palmer kill Angela with Ted's assistance? At last the scene comes and with mounting suspense is played out. There is an offstage shot and the murder victim staggers onstage to die. Is it Palmer? Is it Angela? No, it is Ted. Thus ends the first act, with a coup de théâtre that thwarts all expectations and with no reasonable explanation available for what has happened.

A somewhat similar situation leads up to the ending of the first act of *Program for Murder.* Computer program designer Jeremy has, apparently with the aid of his new computer, Alexis, designed a plot to eliminate Jeremy's wife, Elizabeth, who is threatening, in a nasty divorce settlement, to deprive him of everything, Alexis included. According to the scheme, Alexis will electrocute Elizabeth after Jeremy and his new girl friend and fellow computer buff Brenda leave the house and establish an alibi. When Elizabeth arrives, however, and Brenda has left the room, Jeremy reveals to her that the plot with Brenda was a cover for the real plot, to murder Brenda to gain sole rights to Alexis. In the next scene, as the carefully rehearsed murder plot begins to unroll, the audience is left in suspense as to the identity of the real victim. To further complicate matters, Jeremy's friend Frank unexpectedly arrives, apparently as the result of a misunderstood appointment. Jeremy, shepherding Frank and Elizabeth offstage, seems to decide to abort the plan and surreptitiously asks Brenda to deprogram Alexis while they are out of the room. As she attempts to do so, she is electrocuted. Drawing Elizabeth aside, Jeremy tells her that all has gone according to plan, with Frank providing an unexpected but useful witness to the "accident." Frank, however, who also knows something about computers, may become suspicious of the high voltage wiring attached to Alexis, so Jeremy asks Elizabeth to disconnect the main cable while he distracts Frank. When Elizabeth attempts to do so, she also is electrocuted. The apparently contradictory plots were illusions. Jeremy was in fact setting up both murders.

Anne Ubersfeld has suggested (following such structural analysts of narrative as Propp and Greimas) the analysis of dramatic plots in terms of the structural "roles" played by the characters ("giver," "receiver," "opponent," etc.). If we apply this sort of analysis to the plots of comedy thrillers, we find that a great deal of the confusion and the surprise in such plays comes once again from a conscious subversion of traditional reading expectations. We are trained, not only in detective fiction but in all traditional narratives, to seek a pattern of relationships in which the individual characters, or actants, continue to relate to one another, and to the narrative as a whole, in fairly predictable ways. In the comedy thriller, we might say that actantial roles are cut loose from the actants, so that one can never be sure, from scene to scene, who will be playing any particular actantial role. The "typical" triangle situation would suggest a husband and wife, one of whom conspires with a lover to bring about the death of the other. Because this is so typical, it is frequently suggested in these plays, only to be subverted by some other hidden arrangement—husband and wife's lover against wife, or wife and husband's lover against husband, husband and wife against lover, or even husband against both lover and wife. In some cases, as we have seen, the subversion may be more radical still; a character may seemingly step outside the actantial relationships entirely, to claim recognition as an "actor" on another level of reality altogether.

In traditional detective fiction, the detective is, of course, the central figure, and although theorists of the genre have differed somewhat in assessing his function, there is general agreement that his function is the re-establishment of order in a world put into disorder by the act of murder. Most commonly, the superior intellect of the detective is seen as an exultation of bourgeois scientific rationalism, a demonstration, as Grella observes, that human reason can be relied upon to ensure stability and harmony in "a benevolent and knowable universe."[12] Slavoj Žižek argues for a close relationship between the detective and the psychoanalytic analyst, the "person supposed to know," a "guarantor of meaning" in whose presence an inchoate, lawless collection of details is integrated into a coherent narrative, reinscribed in the symbolic system.[13] The comedy thriller, however, very frequently presents a world neither benevolent nor knowable, a world that regularly appears as a kind of dark parody of Auden's benevolent detective fictions, with the roles of the combatants precisely reversed. Instead of a universe of morality and rationality controlled by the protagonist detective whose role it is to disentangle the web of illusion and misdirection that disrupts a normally transparent epistemology and protects the antagonist murderer, we encounter a world created and dominated by the antagonist, a world of illusion and misdirection, where nothing presented may be trusted as reality, and where the detective's goal of revealing "the real story" in a linear narrative[14] is constantly challenged by the disruptive desire of this antagonist. Character, language, physical setting, indeed all of the many semiotic systems offered by the theatre, can no longer be regarded as transmitters of information contributing to some coherent message or even to a comprehensible network of signs or signifying systems. They become, rather, the unstable media of exchange that Jameson sees as characteristic of the postmodern, whose signs mark "an essentially conflictual relationship between tricksters,"[15] the central trickster being the illusion-creating murderer, engaged in a battle of wits not with the detective, but with the audience. Of the various forms of postmodern anti-detective novel described by Stefano Tani, the comedy thriller is thus clearly closest to the "metafictional" anti-detective novel in which "the detective is the reader who has to make sense out of an unfinished fiction that has been distorted or cut short by a playful and perverse 'criminal, the writer.'"[16]

Clearly, whatever enjoyment plays of this sort seek to inspire in an audience, it cannot be the enjoyment seemingly sought by traditional detective fiction, with its predictable formulas, its celebration of a world of order and reason, and its rigidly controlled variations. The pleasure offered is surely much more akin to that of the ambiguous, open-ended, and highly self-conscious fictions of postmodernism, and it is to the theory of those fictions that we must turn to find insight into both the organization of and the expected response to such work. Roland Barthes's division of fiction into *textes de désir, textes de plaisir,* and *textes de jouissance* provides a useful orientation. The first type, which includes detective stories along with much other popular literature, and about which Barthes has little to say, refers to fictions that emphasize the linear nature of narrative and are read primarily for the pleasure of reaching the end— Barthes evokes the image of a schoolboy watching a striptease. The *texte de plaisir,* which for Barthes includes the major literary works of the tradition and would, for advocates of the mystery story, include the best traditional work in that genre as well, recognizes the end of the narrative as important in providing a closure, but locates the enjoyment of the text in the devices and diversions that, according to a sophisticated set of rules, fill the space between beginning and end. In the postmodern *texte de jouissance,* which Barthes associates with the new experimental novel in France, the sense of fulfillment, comfort, and plentitude sought by more traditional fictional organizations is replaced by the shock and disequilibrium of a text where anecdote disappears in self-reflexive discourse, and the only hero is the disoriented reader. Here the pleasure of an anticipated end and closure is totally subordinated to a more free-flowing enjoyment of the moment and its open possibilities.[17]

When the antagonist takes control of a theatrical detective narration, this sense of *jouissance* tends to pervade everything— the language, the structure of action, the stability of characterization, and the settings and properties that define the tangible world of the play (the gun loaded with blanks is perhaps the most common property in such dramas). Clearly the detective, the central force for order and authority in the conventional genre, cannot continue to play that role in the comedy thriller. In the majority of these plays, the detective does not even appear. He is replaced in the dynamic of the action by a vague offstage power, "the police," whose role generally is to arrive like Fortinbras when the action is essentially over and deal with the situation that the real players have left.

In the rarer cases, when a detective does appear in these plays, he is usually corrupted in some way by the thriller dynamic. Police Sergeant Scott in *Dead Wrong* seems to pursue his investigations in a conventional manner, but at the end of the play he participates in hiding the real murderer. So does Sergeant Jordan in *Deadly Nightcap* (1986), who emphasizes his turncoat role by leaving the force to become an author of crime literature. Inspector Doppler in *Sleuth* turns out to be the apparent murder victim of the first act returned in disguise. Sergeant Stenning in *Murderer* serves only as a foil in Norman Bartholomew's bizarre plot. Inspector Bowden in *Whodunnit* announces near the end of the last act that he has not "the faintest idea of the killer's identity" and resigns from the case amid the protests of the other characters. The mysterious Superintendent Remick in *Suddenly at Home* (1973) seems to have almost a supernatural ability to ask the right questions, but that is because he is not a detective at all, but an actor sent to entrap Glenn, the plotter-protagonist, by Sam, the man Glenn is trying to frame. Glenn's error is in selecting, as his victim, a detective-story writer whose profession has prepared him for plots of this kind. Sam's introduction early in the play could easily be that of the standard protagonist plotter of a comedy thriller, and it shows why he is such a formidable antagonist for such a plotter:

> MAGGIE: Talking about Sammy—what about this new book of his?
> HELEN: I haven't read it. I don't like thrillers and I certainly can't read Sam's. They're like Sammy, far too devious.
> MAGGIE: *(shocked)* Sammy, devious!
> HELEN: I don't mean devious—devious . . .
> MAGGIE: Well, what do you mean?
> HELEN: Come off it, Maggie! You know perfectly well what I mean! He's a darling, but he's got a mind like a corkscrew.[18]

A particularly elaborate case of a detective entering the "cork-screw" world of the thriller is presented by *Sleight of Hand*. Early in the play we are given conflicting evidence, both physical and verbal, indicating both that the protagonist Paul, a magician, has and has not killed his assistant, Alice, in a failed magic trick. A "detective" arrives with the news that Alice's body has been found and proceeds to interrogate Paul, but the detective's name, Dancer, strikes Paul as odd, not only because his girl friend is a professional dancer, but because of its odd echo at Christmas, when this play occurs, of one of Santa's reindeer. With all this onomastic foregrounding, the experienced viewer[19] is doubtless expected to be suspicious of Dancer, quite possibly associating him with the memorable Detective Doppler in *Sleuth* who similarly arrives to question the protagonist about an ambiguous murder and who is revealed at last to be the presumed victim in disguise.

Paul becomes increasingly suspicious about the "real" identity of his guest, especially after Dancer draws a gun and becomes both more threatening and more irrational. "You're not a policeman, are you? Who are you?" challenges Paul, echoing the confusion of the audience. Dancer seems intent on some sadistic revenge for Alice's death, but his motivation and his relationship to her remain unclear. Trickery, disguise, theatrical turns, and imitation deaths mark the evening-long struggle between Dancer and Paul. The identity of Dancer remains unclear. For a time it seems he might be Alice's brother intent on avenging her death, a role highly appropriate to traditional drama. Later, he seems to be the new lover of Paul's girl friend, Sharon, at work to remove a romantic rival, a role often encountered in comedy thrillers. Not until the end of the play is the truth revealed. He really *is* a detective, and all the play's illusions and misdirections were set up, with Sharon's help, to trick Paul into admitting that he had indeed murdered Alice. "You should have believed the first thing I told you," "Dancer" observes, illustrating a point, made several times in the play, that the ultimate trick is no trick at all. In the subversive world of the comedy thriller, where the audience expects a norm of trickery, truth itself can be used to mislead, since it will be taken to be illusion. In this rare example of a detective achieving a fairly conventional triumph over a murderer, the means are totally unconventional. There is no careful interrogation, no examination of clues, no logical construction of the death event; the detective has triumphed only because he was willing to enter the murderer's world of disguise and misdirection and beat him at his own game. A similar situation may be seen in *An Act of the Imagination*, where Sergeant Burchitt exposes the murderer by engaging in just the sort of theatricalized illusions normally employed by the murderous protagonists in this genre—staging a false death with blanks and even rigging a special wall panel to provide a suitable bloody background for the false event.

Although *Sleight of Hand* is the only play here considered with a magician as protagonist, it is clear that the magician, as a performer, has a very useful affinity to the murderer in a comedy thriller and, by extension, to the author of such a work. Disguise, illusion, misdirection, and mystification are the stock-in-trade of all three. The relationship between the dynamics of the magic show and the thriller we are watching is constantly suggested, even if never openly stated, from the first line, delivered by Paul in an isolated spot: "I'm a conjurer . . . I deal in illusions," to "Dancer's" final line, "no more tricks, the show's over."[20]

The use of a magician protagonist thus foregrounds the ludic element of such a play as well as emphasizing the narrative self-consciousness that contributes so significantly to the parodic flavor of these works. *Sleight of Hand* offers us the only example of a magician protagonist, though Richard Jannings, the protagonist of *Solitary Confinement*, collects Houdini memorabilia, and the major false death in the play involves Jannings escaping from a trunk presumably used by the famous magician. Furthermore, Keach, creator of Jannings, has described *Solitary Con-*

finement as "more a magic show than a mystery."[21] Many of the comedy thrillers contain characters who are actors, and almost all of them take advantage of their professional skills, as does the magician, to mislead their fellows and, it is hoped, the audience with misdirection, trick properties, and disguises. They are also quick to make observations about the convergence of the theatre and their own world. Actors make up most of the cast of *The Butler Did It* and *Whodunnit* and are central figures in *Corpse, Murder among Friends, Stage Struck,* and *Fatal Attraction.* In a number of other plays, leading characters, even though not actors, consciously "theatricalize" their situations by appearing in disguise, committing false murders with blank guns, staging elaborate hoaxes, and so on.

Readers and writers of detective fiction are sometimes found as characters in non-dramatic examples of such fiction. Ariadne Oliver, who appears in several of Christie's Hercule Poirot stories, is one of the best known of these. Inevitably, such characters introduce at least some element of generic self-consciousness and reflexivity. This occasional feature of standard detective fiction becomes a far more central device, however, in the comedy thrillers, many of whose protagonists are, like their creators, authors of thrillers or of detective fiction. Typical is the successful writer who decides to apply his literary skills to real crime, making him a special type of character, a kind of co-creator, with the actual author, of the dramatic action. As this book is being written, a new play has just opened in London, though not, alas, yet seen by this author, called *Murder by Misadventure,* written by Edward Taylor. It features, I believe for the first time, *two* mystery writers as antagonists, former collaborators on TV mysteries, who have had a falling out and decide to use their expertise to set up each other's murder. The effect of the mystery writer, as protagonist, on the dramatic action will be the concern of a later chapter.

Not surprisingly, the actors and authors so often found in the casts of comedy thrillers are well aware of the close relationship between their activities in the "real" world of the play and those of the "fictional" characters they professionally create and the similarity of the world they inhabit to that constructed for detective fiction. Dramatic writers for centuries have sought to excuse some of the more unlikely developments in their narratives by having a character give some variation of the remark, "if I were to see this in a play, I would not believe it." The device is now so well-worn that, if anything, it calls attention to itself as a device and thus, ironically, reinforces rather than reduces the consciousness of fictionality. Still, this very exhaustion of the trope allows the comedy thriller author to use it parodically, as a part of a total structure of generic reflexivity. The mysterious character, Stone, in Richard Harris's *The Business of Murder* (1981) confronts a writer of murder plays with the hall-of-mirrors line: "People don't behave like me, do they? Only in plays. But you're not a character in a play, Miss Redmon, you're only too real. You sit down and work out your plots . . . so why shouldn't I?"[22]

When the murderer/protagonist who sets up the action of a thriller is also the author of detective fiction, it is hardly surprising that he or she would be aware of the theatrical, or at least the constructed nature of his or her activity, but other characters may come to a similar insight about the world they inhabit, especially if they are avid readers of detective fiction. The complex murder plot of mystery writer Selwyn Piper in *Murder by the Book* is almost immediately seen through by Peter Fletcher, the bright young man from the next-door apartment, but this is hardly surprising, since, as Peter himself explains:

> I've been a Piper fan for years. I always put the book down just before the last chapter, then I pop into bed and lie awake until I've worked it out. Then I get up and finish it to see if I was right.[23]

The amateur reader of detective fiction who, for that reason, is more perceptive than the police in seeing through a complex plot is a character not infrequently encountered in such fiction, both in novels and on stage. Susan, in A. A. Milne's *The Perfect Alibi* (1928), is a typical example. She begins the play reading a detective story and ends it by exposing the villains. In the comedy thriller, even the police have begun to realize that a solid grounding in detective fiction is the best preparation for solving the sort of crime they encounter in these plays. An interchange in Shaffer's *Whodunnit* makes clear this concern:

> INSPECTOR: You know a bit about detective fiction then, do you, Sergeant?
>
> SERGEANT: Oh, yes, sir. I read a lot of them myself. My favorite is Hercule Poirot *(French accent)* ze little grey cells . . . you know, sir.
>
> INSPECTOR: I prefer Dr. Fell myself . . . a more erudite class of fellow altogether.
>
> SERGEANT: Oh yes, I know him—he's in the John Dickson Carr books, isn't he?
>
> INSPECTOR: That's right. A whopping great fellow who wheezes about on a cane, wearing a big cloak, floppy hat, smokes cigars, drinks quarts of beer, quoting funny bits of poetry. I think he was based a bit on that writer fellow G. K. Chesterton.
>
> SERGEANT: Really, sir?
>
> INSPECTOR: Yes. In another life I often fancy I'd have been a bit like that.
>
> SERGEANT: I wouldn't have thought you'd read all those thrillers, sir.
>
> INSPECTOR: I must admit I'm something of a fan myself.

This passage of generic commentary has a strong bearing on the development of the play's action, since the characteristics of the crime being investigated strike the police as clearly more appropriate to the "world of thriller fiction" than to that of normal reality. "If I'm to solve this crime," the inspector at last concludes, "I've got to put myself into the position of the person who designed it. In other words I should try and behave a bit like one of those eccentric sleuths out of detective fiction. It might just give me the proper insights." Accordingly, he decides that he will interrogate the suspects in the manner of one of John Dickson Carr's fictional detectives. He "selects a floppy hat, a cape and puts them on. From a nearby umbrella stand he selects a cane and by the time he descends the stairs again he is 'Doctor Fell,' limp and all."[24]

The inspector's selection of Carr's Dr. Fell as a model (rather than, for example, Hercule Poirot, Inspector Maigret, or Sherlock Holmes) is a revealing choice that, not surprisingly, seems to echo the proclivities of the Inspector's own creator, Anthony Shaffer. Shaffer's *Sleuth*, in many ways a key work in defining the modern comedy thriller, features a detective story writer, Andrew Wyke, who is not, like Inspector Bowden, a devoted reader of Carr's works, but an affectionate parody of Carr himself. The play opens with Wyke sitting at his desk reading aloud the bizarre solution to his latest "locked-room" mystery:

> "As you appear to know so much, Lord Merridew, sir," said the Inspector, "I wonder if you could explain just how the murderer managed to leave the body in the middle of the tennis court, and effect his escape without leaving any tracks behind him in the red dust. Frankly, sir, we in the Police Force are just plain baffled." St. John Lord Merridew, the great detective, rose majestically, his huge Father Christmas face glowing with mischievous delight. Slowly he brushed the crumbs of seedy cake from the folds of his pendulous waistcoat. "The police may be baffled, Inspector," he boomed, "but Merridew is not. It's altogether a question of a little research and a little ratiocination. Thirty years ago, the murderer, Doctor Grayson, was a distinguished member of the Ballet Russe dancing under the name of Oleg Graysinski. The years may have altered his appearance, but his old skill had not deserted him. He carried the body out to the centre of the tennis court, walking on his points along the white tape which divided the service boxes. From there he threw it five feet into the court, towards the base line, where it was found, and then, with a neatly executed fouette, faced about and returned the way he had come, thus leaving no traces."[25]

The audience member who has read Carr's novels will immediately recognize this cunning parody. Seemingly inexplicable circumstances, a befuddled police officer, and a smug and superior private detective possessing the requisite esoteric knowledge—these, of course, are classic features of the genre. But Carr's special variations on these are also lovingly reproduced—the grotesque Merridew, with his huge bulk, his "father Christmas face," even the crumbs on his waistcoat, is physically, verbally, and intellectually an unmistakable blend of Carr's Dr. Fell and Sir Henry Merrivale. The situation, and its bizarre solution, closely duplicates the sort of locked-room puzzle that was Carr's specialty, and indeed the "tennis court" mystery, much as described here, was the centerpiece of one of Carr's Dr. Fell mysteries—*The Problem of the Wire Cage* (1944).[26]

Shaffer's decision to stress a relationship to Carr rather than, for example, to Conan Doyle or to Christie seems clearly more than a matter of personal preference. In terms of the tradition of detective fiction, the world of the comedy thriller is in fact much closer to that of Carr than to that of any other well-known contributor to this genre. In Carr's work we find similar challenges to epistemological stability, often the result of plots of enormous ingenuity and complexity made more complex still by the workings of counterplots or the erratic intervention of chance, what one of Carr's detectives regularly characterizes as "the general cussedness of things." Here also we find a pushing of the genre to the verge of self-destruction, as in the taunting footnotes to the reader in *The Nine Wrong Answers* (1952) or in the chillingly appropriate but generically extremely subversive final chapter to *The Burning Court* (1937). And, perhaps most striking of all, we find, in Carr's *The Three Coffins* (1935), a passage of generic self-reflexivity so striking as to have stimulated a special appendix in Champigny's treatise on detective fiction, *What Will Have Happened* (1977). In this passage, Inspector Bowden's hero, Dr. Fell, introduces a lecture on a favorite concern of his creator, the locked-room mystery. The situation is thus highly self-conscious, but the lecture soon becomes much more so:

> "I will now lecture," said Dr. Fell inexorably, "on the general mechanics and development of the situation which is known in detective fiction as the 'hermetically sealed chamber.' Harrumph. All those opposing can skip this chapter. Harrumph. To begin with, gentlemen! Having been improving my mind with sensational fiction for the last forty years, I can say—"
>
> "But, if you're going to analyze impossible situations," interrupted Pettis, "why discuss detective fiction?"
>
> "Because," said the Doctor, frankly, "we're in a detective story, and we don't fool the reader by pretending we're not. Let's not invent excuses to drag in a discussion of detective stories. Let's candidly glory in the noblest pursuits possible to characters in a book."[27]

Champigny calls this kind of self-awareness of a fictional character rare, but not unique, and offers Pirandello as another example. The connection is a reasonable one, though it is somewhat misleading. Moving from a novel to a dramatic text raises new questions in terms of character self-awareness that considerably complicate such references. Champigny is able to conclude his analysis of the Dr. Fell passage by observing that, despite its apparent integration of a free element within the fictional world, "this integration is only a semblance," and the passage, though more original, remains a literary construct of the "dear-reader-our-heroine type."[28] Earlier, however, Champigny contrasts Dr. Fell's statement with that of an actor who could say, "I am Hamlet," distinguishing himself as a player of that role. "Attributed to the actor, not to the character," Champigny observes, "the fictionalizing operator would thus recover its transcendence."[29]

Indeed, it is precisely on the level of this operation that Pirandello and the writers of modern mystery thrillers often develop a kind of actantial and generic self-awareness, impossible in the novel, through the "double-coding" of narrative text and the more open possibilities offered by performance. "Dr. Fell" can claim, correctly, to be within a fictive universe, but he can only do so within the confines of that universe. "Inspector Bowden," like a Pirandello character, can in fact escape his fictive universe through performance, appearing in the "real world" of, for example, the curtain calls or direct interaction with the audience. Whether this results in a "fictionalizing" of the performance situation or a "making transcendent" of Bowden, or a kind of uneasy combination of the two, it is a strategy of subversion uniquely available to theatre.

Umberto Eco has described the phenomenon of acting as being based upon two different speech acts:

> The first one is performed by the actor who is making a performative statement—"I am acting." By this implicit statement the actor tells the truth since he announces that *from that moment on* he will lie. The second one is represented by a pseudo-statement where the subject of the statement is already the character, not the actor . . . Because of the first performative act, everything following it becomes referentially opaque. Through the decision of the performer ("I am another man") we enter the possible world of performance, a world of lies in which we are entitled to celebrate the suspension of disbelief.[30]

While this is true of the conventional theatre experience, especially in the realistic tradition, it is also true that, despite the operation of Eco's first performative statement, there is always some consciousness on the part of both performer and audience of a "reality" behind the "lie" of acting. The performance is never really "referentially opaque," even when both *pretend* that it is so. And, of course, a dramatist like Pirandello may decide to foreground this phenomenon by suggesting that actors, from time to time, claim to renounce their first performative statement, thereby offering an apparent referential grounding for the pseudo-statements that follow. The normal actor-audience contract is thus placed in continual renegotiation, with the ontological status of any specific speech act called into question.

Since the goal of the comedy thriller is to keep surprising its audiences with new variation of a form that, even in its surprises, moves always toward codification, this interplay of reality and theatre has continued to be the area of increasingly elaborate and complex development. Just as the "settings" of mystery thrillers often suggest that the audience remember that they are not really rooms, but theatrical constructions, so the characters that inhabit these rooms are often presented so as to foreground, for spectators, Eco's first speech act, "I am acting," as much as any of the subsequent statements that are interpretively based upon it.

4 MURDER BY THE BOOK

> "I conceived the whole thing as though it were my latest thriller."
> —Selwyn in *Murder by the Book*

Ira Levin's *Deathtrap* opens with a writer of dramatic thrillers, Sidney Bruhl, reading a new script. His first line begins—"*Deathtrap.* A thriller in two acts. One set, five characters. A juicy murder in Act One, unexpected developments in Act Two."[1] The audience is at once placed in a world of the postmodern whose artistic expression, as Charles Newman suggests, involves "a commentary on the aesthetic history of whatever genre it adopts."[2] Bruhl's opening line is also, of course, a commentary on the reception of that genre and, perhaps most importantly, on the immediate experience of the audience in its encounter with this particular play. Even more radical is the opening of *Accomplice* where a character enters, mixes a drink, and then remarks, "that's *exactly* how all these *plays* begin, isn't it?" and proceeds to quote the description of the scene he is in and the stage directions for the pantomime he has just performed. Surely there is a close, operative similarity between such opening gambits and the opening sentence of Calvino's postmodernist novel, *If on a winter's night a traveler* (1981): "You are about to begin reading Italo Calvino's new novel, *If on a winter's night a traveler*."[3]

Silvio Gaggi and Linda Hutcheon, among others, have emphasized the centrality of self-referentiality in all postmodern art, and both have mentioned the detective story as a genre particularly open to self-referential narration, both overt and covert.[4] Characters in detective novels and plays are often readers of, and sometimes even writers of, such fiction. When amateur detectives step in to solve the crime, as they often do, their procedures and their conclusions are frequently based upon a long practice of reading mystery fiction. I have already remarked on how often the protagonist of the modern comedy thriller is himself a writer of mystery fiction, and the action of the play we are seeing is, for him, a professional activity. I use the male pronoun advisedly since, despite the prominence of women authors in this genre, these author/protagonists in comedy thrillers are almost invariably male, reflecting the authorship of the thrillers themselves. To date, the comedy thriller, unlike other detective fiction, including stage works, has attracted only male authors. This may help to explain what seem to be general assumptions in the genre about the comparative activity in plotting of men and women. While women are occasionally recognized as possible authors of crime fiction, they do not seem to be often tempted, as their male counterparts are, to use their imagination to plan real murders. Nor, on the whole, do they seem to be as interested, even in the process of plotting, as the males. The difference is spelled out specifically in Frederick Knott's *Write Me a Murder* (1961), when the would-be author, Julie, informs her future partner in crime, David, that she is excellent on character but has problems with story. David crystallizes the conventional male position: "I'm the other way 'round. It just amuses me to work out a plot. You should try a murder story some time. Good exercise in construction."[5] When a man and woman work out a murder plot in these plays, it is almost invariably the man who takes the initiative, both in planning and in execution.

The disappearance of the stabilizing detective and the foregounding of the destabilizing murderer in modern comedy thrillers is so central that, though detective fiction authors are perhaps the most common type of protagonist in such plays, there is not a single example of such a protagonist utilizing the skills he has developed in his fiction to attempt the solution of a real crime (as for example, Arthur Conan Doyle did). On the contrary, in every case these skills are utilized for planning a perfect murder, in which illusion and deception invariably play an important part. In the traditional detective drama, when the protagonist was the detective, the unknown murderer normally controlled the mysterious events of the first part of the play and the detective those of the later part, which often included a theatricalized re-enactment of the murder scene itself. Thus, the detective served as a kind of co-creator, with the actual author of the piece, of the re-stabilized world in which the illusions of the murderer were exposed and truth and justice achieved. In the comedy thriller, the actual author has formed an alliance, as co-creator, with the murderer, whose activities are not only foregrounded but whose world of misdirection and illusion controls the entire play.

The most important result of this new alliance is to make the play of reality and fictionality a constant concern in these plays, not only for the audiences, but frequently for the characters themselves. I will return presently to some discussion of this concern, but first we might note that the new alliance has not only important thematic and philosophical consequences but also requires significant changes in the organization of the dramatic action. The new comedy thrillers have not, on the most basic level, departed from the givens of the traditional mystery play. They are still built around the commission of a murder and the revelation of its perpetrator, and indeed opening act suspense often relies heavily upon an audience assumption that sooner or later someone is going to be murdered. Ordean Haugen's introduction to the mystery play somewhat whimsically evokes the conventions of this genre:

> Suddenly the lights go out, and there is a hushed silence. Then a shot breaks the quiet of the night, followed by a harrowing scream. When the lights come on, a body lies in full view of the audience. Now they can breathe easier again, sit back and relax. The show is on.[6]

The exact placement of this pivotal event in the narrative presents a problem, both in the detective story and its theatrical equivalent. As Haugen suggests, the show is really not "on" until the murder is committed, and both readers and spectators may well become impatient if this expected event is too long postponed. On the other hand, there is usually a certain amount of necessary contextualization to be imparted before the murder can be properly experienced as a meaningful event in a narrative structure, and so some delay is necessary. Although novels of detection vary widely on this matter, mystery plays have developed a standard pattern so common that audiences have come to build it into the pattern of generic expectations.

Stoppard's *The Real Inspector Hound* notwithstanding, murder plays rarely, if ever, actually begin with a corpse on the stage, however much the audience may wish to move quickly to that point. Glines's *Murder in Disguise*, not actually a comedy thriller but utilizing some of that subgenre's tongue-in-cheek self-consciousness, begins with two characters on stage, one talking to the other who is slumped in his chair with a knife in his chest. A chuckle from the audience as the curtain opens shows that they have become, by the 1990s, sufficiently comfortable with subversions of the crime genre to recognize this as a parodaic image, and, indeed, the knife is soon revealed as a prop for a proposed "murder game." Normally in a murder play, a good deal of preliminary ground must be covered before the murder is actually committed—setting up the situation, building a sense of tension and foreboding, introducing the characters and, very likely, scattering strong hints about their motives or potential for committing the invariable, upcoming crime. The actual murder, committed in darkness or at least in such a manner that the audience does not know the identity of the murderer, comes at the peak of this building tension and almost inevitably provides a climax to a scene or an act. The police can then be called during the scene or act break, and the next act or scene can begin with the detective on the scene and ready to begin his investigations. Christie's *Toward Zero* provides a useful, typical example of this with a bonus in the form of a modestly self-reflexive passage that hints at the far greater generic self-consciousness of later comedy thrillers. After the family and acquaintances, who will later provide the victim and usual suspects, have been introduced and the first act draws to an end, the character, Treves, finds another character, Royde, reading a detective story. "Always seems to me these yarns begin in the wrong place," Royde observes. "Begin with the murder. But the murder's not really the beginning. . . . As I see it, the real story begins long before—years before sometimes. Most do. All the causes and events that bring the people concerned to a certain place at a certain time. And then, over the top—zero hour." The image strikes Treves, who compliments Royde on his observation and repeats, musing: "All sorts of people converging towards a given spot and hour—all going toward zero (He pauses briefly) Toward Zero." The two men look at each other as the act ends.[7] The murder in this play does not occur until the end of the first scene in the second act, the second scene beginning, according to convention, with the arrival of the police.

Although modern comedy thrillers very frequently follow the conventional structure found in mystery dramas of the *Toward Zero* type, by placing a murder at the climax of an early act or scene, the material preceding the murder is radically different, reflecting the fact that in most of these thrillers, as in the crime plays of the early nineteenth century, the murderer is known from the beginning. The careful presentation of a group of potential suspects and the establishment of their relationships, providing an introduction to the long-running "real story" that interests Royde and that will very likely also occupy the attention of the play's detective, is here unnecessary, since we normally know, very early, both the murderer and the motive. What we are often given instead is the careful rehearsal of an alibi involving, as it almost invariably does, a series of actions leading up to and immediately following the murder, then a new source of surprise and suspense is introduced. Instead of filling the time leading up to the actual murder with ominous, but necessarily vague, threats and premonitions and with a potentially rather uninteresting introduction of all the suspects and their backgrounds, the dramatist can set up a very specific plot and center the interest on whether it will succeed.

This switch from the identity of the murderer to the success of his plot was in fact specifically suggested as a new strategy in a 1958 mystery play, Arthur Watkin's *Not in the Book,* which anticipates a number of the strategies of the more complex comedy thrillers of the 1970s and 1980s. In it a young author has written what he calls a "howdunnit," as opposed to the familiar "whodunnit." In a "howdunnit," he explains, "there's no mystery about the murderer. The reader knows who he is and is asked to watch him at work." The distinction, though I believe it is not found outside this play, is a useful one, and we might classify many of the comedy thrillers we are examining as "howdunnits" rather than "whodunnits." If the audience is aware in advance of the details of the murderer's plot, especially if it is a rather complex one, then much suspense can be generated when specific details of the plan do not work out as expected, and a very pleasurable tension can be maintained as the protagonist must hastily improvise to keep developments on track. This is a formula that has also been utilized with great success in the elaborate robbery plans that form the basis of the "caper" movies and novels.

Although "howdunnits" were much less common, when Watkin's play appeared, than the traditional "whodunnits," his young author had by no means hit upon a totally new approach. In his study of nineteenth- and early twentieth-century melodrama, Frank Rahill provides a brief history of the murder mystery play up until the early 1940s. He observes that in the early 1930s several British authors departed in an interesting manner from the "whodunnit" formula that had been developed, up to that point, largely in America. In such works as A. A. Milne's *The Perfect Alibi* (1928), D. N. Rubin's *Riddle-Me-This* (1930) and Anthony Armstrong's *Ten-Minute Alibi* (1933), "the crime is committed early in the play before the eyes of the audience, and an alibi is carefully rehearsed in full view on the stage. The loss entailed in this sacrifice of the surprise ending proves trifling and the gain immense. The thrill of the chase is no less keen for the quarry's being known, and the opportunities for characterization are vastly enlarged."[8]

Not all of these plays actually made much of their unusual approach. Rubin's *Riddle-Me-This,* after its unconventional opening scene, followed so conventional a detection structure that the program had to include a special note, "For the Benefit of the Late-Comer," advising them that "this is not a mystery play. In the opening Scene we saw Dr. Tindal commit the murder and arrange evidence to entrap an innocent man."[9]

Despite the intriguing self-reflexivity of its London title, *The Fourth Wall,* A. A. Milne's *The Perfect Alibi* is in fact even more conventional. At the end of the first act we see the murder committed by two murderers working in concert. Their plan is not an extremely elaborate one, and we do not see it set up in advance. Nor does it encounter any major obstacles. The policeman, whom they expected to come by bicycle, in fact uses a motorbike, which causes them to speed up their activities a bit, but does not appear to interfere seriously with their plot. As the police investigation takes place during the second act, we find that they have developed rather complex alibis that depend on each other for confirmation, alibis that convince the investigating officer. In the final act, the two young lovers of the play, readers of detective fiction, figure out the crime and the alibi and trick one of the murderers into a confession. Practically speaking, the first-act murder could have taken place off stage, depriving the audience of the knowledge of its perpetrators, and the subsequent acts would create much the same effect, since the crime is reconstructed in traditional fashion by clever amateurs in the final act anyway.

In *Ten-Minute Alibi*, however, a much less conventional pattern of action is developed, one much more suggestive of future experimentation, despite the ties of its basic situation to traditional melodrama. The young hero, Colin, seems unable to prevent the plans of the villain, Sevilla, to carry off the naive heroine, Betty. After the opening scene, however, the plot takes an unusual turn. Colin falls asleep and we see him in his dream murdering Sevilla and juggling Sevilla's clock to establish himself an alibi. Seeing no other way to save Betty, Colin decides to convert the dream into reality, and in the second act, plagued constantly by tension-producing, unexpected developments, he eventually manages to carry out the murder. Certainly, as Rahill suggests, the "thrill of the chase" is not diminished in this play by our knowledge of the murderer's identity, since we tend to sympathize with Colin and wonder, as the investigation goes on, whether he will get away with his crime. But there is also a new sort of tension in the early part of the play, as we wonder, through a series of unexpected obstacles, whether the murder can in fact be successfully committed. In later plays, this sort of tension between an elaborate plot and its execution often becomes much more central to the dynamics of the drama than the traditional pursuit of the murderer.

Since Colin is filling the role of the traditional young hero, the use of the dream sequence is probably designed to allow him to plot the murder without quite taking responsibility for it. In later plays, when audiences and authors are quite comfortable with protagonists drawn in darker hues who can revel in their plotting rather than having it creep upon them almost unawares, such an awkward device is no longer necessary. Indeed, the dynamic of audience sympathy becomes much more subversive. Although we may condemn Colin's decision to murder Sevilla on general moral grounds, our condemnation is obviously tempered by the fact that Colin is identified with the traditional hero's role and Sevilla with the traditional villain's. The protagonists in the comedy thrillers usually have no such heroic cast. The most common form of this trope shows a married writer deciding to apply the strategies he has honed in fiction in the "real life" of the dramatic world to rid himself of an unwanted spouse or of a younger, more romantic, sexual rival. The murders they commit are for personal advantage and their characters often much closer to that of the traditional villain than of the hero. Our sympathies for them are engaged not on the level of their goal, but on the level of our fascination of their plotting.

Write Me a Murder can be seen as a kind of transitional piece toward this darker and more plot-driven world. Its leading figures, Julie and David, are certainly more sympathetic than Julie's manipulative husband, Charles, and there is much more a sense that they are trapped by events rather than that they are manipulating them. Charles plans to buy an English estate for speculation. His wife is writing a murder story but having trouble with its plotting, and she seeks the help of David, the present owner of the estate, who is interested in such matters. Gradually, as the story develops and they become more attracted to each other, they see the story as a possible blueprint for the death of the obnoxious Charles. In a highly effective coup de théâtre, however, the very evening that they have all of the elements of the plot in place, Charles is killed in an automobile accident.

A year passes and Julie and David, now married, return to the estate. Their happiness, however, encounters a new threat, the return of David's black sheep brother, Clive, from abroad, who is apparently determined to be a part of their future plans. While Julie is away in London, David recalls the murder plot and uses it to dispose of Clive. Soon after, Julie arrives, but so does Scotland Yard. She too has remembered the story and submitted it to a newspaper contest where it won first prize and was printed, the same day the murder was committed. The ironic interplay of fictional and real murder and the surprising turn of the unexpected, but perfectly timed, death of the husband suggest some of the strategies of later comedy thrillers, but despite its self-reflexive concerns, the assumptions and values of *Write Me a Murder* remain essentially traditional. We are never misled, as we are continually in recent comedy thrillers, about what is reality and what is fiction, and equally importantly, the manipulations of the plotters take place in a moral universe where, even if the police might be misled, poetic justice (in the most literal and also the most ironic sense of the phrase) guarantees the exposure of the truth.

The same moral stability underlies the universe of Jack Popplewell's *Dead on Nine* (1956), though its subject, a mystery writer plotting his wife's murder, and its foregrounding of a fiction/reality tension and tone of ironic self-consciousness provides many hints of later, more radical works. The opening act continually conflates the real-life situation of the characters with the mystery play Robert is writing. Robert's wife, Esmeralda, tells his secretary, Marion, that she will not divorce him. When a friend, Tom, arrives, Marion passes this off, with genders reversed, as a discussion of the second act of the new play:

> MARION (*glancing at Esmeralda*) In Mr. Leigh's play the husband is not in love with his wife. He loathes her. He doesn't want her for herself. He still won't let her go.
> TOM: Why the hell not if he doesn't want her?
> ESMERALDA: Not everybody approves of divorce, you know.[10]

Soon after this coded conversation, Marion leaves and Tom reveals to Esmeralda that he is attracted to her. Their conversation reverts again to the presumed situation of Robert's play:

> TOM: You and Robert don't get on. Why?
> ESMERALDA: We bore each other.
> TOM: What are you doing about it?
> ESMERALDA: Nothing.
> TOM: What's he doing?
> ESMERALDA: *(looking directly at him)* What can he do?
> TOM: Well, he can . . . *(He breaks off)*
> ESMERALDA: Yes?
> TOM: *(quickly)* I was going to say you could get a divorce. *(He goes on as if in the same sentence)* That's what you said his play was about, didn't you?
> ESMERALDA: Isn't it a coincidence?
> TOM: Only you said two men and one woman. And this is . . .
> ESMERALDA: Two women and one man?
> TOM: Who's the other woman?
> ESMERALDA: *(smiling)* Who would it be?
> TOM: So he is doing someting about it after all. *(He puts his glass on the desk)*
> *(There is a flash of lightning off)*[11]

We hardly need the ubiquitous flash of lightning to alert us to the generic self-consciousness of this exchange. In the complex plotting and counter-plotting that follow, Tom and Marion, the outside lovers, are both killed, and though Robert and Esmeralda have arranged for alibis that the play's clever detective suspects but cannot break, he outwits them by building a case against each for the *other* crime, for which they have no alibi. So crime is punished, order restored, and the traditional intellectual supremacy of the detective reaffirmed. The victory is a narrow one, though, and the detective triumphs not by establishing truth in the traditional manner but by entering the villain's world of constructed truth and besting him there at his own game. We are here very close to the triumph of that world of constructed truth as we see it commonly assumed in more recent examples of the genre.

In a sense, the traditional detective drama, at least in its later parts, takes us inside the mind of the detective, or at least into a world whose restored order reflects the order of that mind, while the modern thriller takes us into the mind of, or into a world reflecting the ludic instability of the mind of, the plotter of murder. The mind of the mystery writer provides an ideal locus for the interplay of the world of imagination and the world of reality, and a few early twentieth-century thrillers, from *Seven Keys to Baldpate* (1913) to *Ask Me No Questions* (1948), mystified their audiences by actually placing the action within the author's mind as the plot was being worked out. In *Seven Keys to Baldpate*, a night of complex and confusing incidents involving a young man attempting to write a mystery fiction and a group of people very much like those he normally utilized in his novels ends with the revelation that everything we have been seeing was in fact the fiction that he was writing. *Ask Me No Questions*, by Lee Edwards, plays a similar game in a more modern way. A well-known mystery novelist consults a psychiatrist about a frightening situation the novelist faces. The entire play is a flashback showing how the novelist and his fiancée became involved in a series of murders, playing the typical couple of amateur detectives who spot the murderer at considerable threat to themselves. The final scene, however, reveals that all of this was a fiction, the plot of a new novel, that its author wanted to test out on the doctor for psychological verisimilitude.

The theatre is a narrative genre particularly adaptable to this sort of trickery, since the physical presence of its means gives a kind of authenticity to the most imaginary events. In a novel, if Perry merely told his story to the doctor, it would be much easier to recall that it was a story and, therefore, very likely "fictionalized" to some extent by its teller. In the theatre, however, once we move to the physical representation of the flashback, the narrator disappears from our consciousness, and we seem to be direct witnesses of an unmediated reality. The theatre has, of course, long played with this phenomenon, especially in those periods that, like our own, were very self-conscious about the apparatus of artistic representation. Corneille's *L'Illusion Comique* (1636) plays a similar but even more complex game with the audience than *Ask Me No Questions*. Pridamant, whose son, Clindor, has been missing for ten years, consults a magician who conjures up visions of the son's activities that take up most of the play. The loves and death of the son are shown, much to the sorrow of the father, but a final vision shows the son and colleagues counting out money. The son has in fact become a successful actor, and the loves and death we witnessed showed him pursuing his profession. The "theatrical illusion" allows neither us nor his father to distinguish between real and mimetic actions the son may be performing.

The device of placing the audience, without warning, inside the imagination of the protagonist has not been frequently employed in the modern comedy thriller, probably because it is less flexible in its continuing destabilization of the dramatic world than devices embedded in the "reality" of that world, such as disguises and theatrical "stagings" by some characters to mislead others (and the audience). I am aware of only one recent play where the device of the imagined action is central, Richard Levinson and William Link's *Guilty Conscience*, and it is noteworthy that in this play the device, far from being utilized as a single trick played at the end to provide a satisfactory explanation for the entire mysterious activity of the play, is played with, and indeed subverted throughout, the action. The protagonist here is a famous criminal lawyer, not a mystery author, but he nevertheless constructs fictional fantasies about the "perfect murder" of his wife. The play's opening soliloquy begins "What if . . . *(He blows a plume of smoke toward the ceiling)* What if I hired someone to kill her? *(He plays with it in his mind)*."[12] He considers and rejects the hit man and an "accidental" fire in this opening meditation before his wife appears and interrupts his daydreams. Later, an invitation to speak at a dinner gives him an idea for an alibi. The next scene shows him killing his wife and leaving evidence to suggest a burglar. A shift in lighting, not in the set, takes us into a courtroom where a clever prosecutor finds a series of holes in the lawyer's story. Finally Arthur, the lawyer, breaks off the scene irritably: "All right, it won't work." We return to the set and lighting of the opening scene. All this has been a mental spinning out of one of Arthur's murder plots and its consequences. Structurally speaking, we are now where *Seven Keys to Baldpate* and *Ask Me No Questions* ended, with the revelation of the fictionality of what we have been witnessing. In *Guilty Conscience*, however, we are only somewhat past the middle of the first act. Clearly there are many tricks yet to be played.

As the act progresses, we meet Arthur's secret girl friend, Jackie, and see him fantasize about several more death scenarios for his wife, though now the convention is familiar and no attempt is made to portray these as anything other than products of Arthur's imagination. As he surfaces from the last of these, however, he, and we, are astonished to find Louise, his wife, leveling a gun at him. So ends the first act. The first scene of the second act is set two days earlier, and we see Louise and Jackie meeting, exchanging information, and deciding to murder Arthur. In the self-reflexive domain of the comedy thriller, so astonishing a turn is not at all uncommon. On the contrary, an elaborate murder plot set up by a protagonist husband is quite often reflected by an equally elaborate murder plot set up by his projected victim, as in the parallel plots of Palmer and Ted against Angela, and Angela and Ted against Palmer, set up in the first act of Bob Barry's *Murder among Friends*. Such activity establishes a structural hall of mirrors that contributes importantly to the artificiality and playfulness of this fictive world. It also provides the women characters in these plays a chance finally to demonstrate their own ability as plotters, and in the most recent examples (possibly in part to upset generic expectations) they often prove superior to the men.

In *Guilty Conscience,* the flashback to the women's plotting is followed by a return to Louise menacing Arthur with the gun. Apparently, the plot is proceeding as planned. But Arthur begins to project what will happen at the trial and proves Louise's plan as full of problems as his own. Having thwarted his wife's plan, Arthur is about to leave to meet a new mistress when Louise scuffles with him and, in the confusion, is shot. Another court scene follows in which Arthur is found guilty of murder, but this scene dissolves back to him dreaming in his chair. He observes wryly: "It would probably serve me right . . . Not that either one of them would seriously consider murdering me— although God knows what they'd do if they met each other. *(slight smile)* Or if they knew about Gail."[13] The entire middle section of the play, flashback included, is thus revealed to be yet another daydream, not the return to "reality" suggested in the first act. Nor is this the play's final turn, though we are now only two pages from the end. In the earlier versions, the "crimes" were revealed as fictive illusions, and this revelation returned us to a world of health and sanity. Not so *Guilty Conscience.* Arthur starts to leave the room and is shot by Louise, who then calls Jackie to establish her alibi. The counterplot Arthur imagined in fact existed, and the play ends with Louise creating evidence of a burglary around his body. As is often the case in modern comedy thrillers, the police have never arrived, and the assumption is that when they do, they will accept the constructed scene as reality.

While it is true that in the theatre, what seems to be reality may turn out to be illusion, it is equally true, as Arthur discovers too late in *Guilty Conscience,* that what seems to be illusion may turn out to be reality. It is this second possibility that is much more likely to occupy the mystery writer protagonists of modern comedy thrillers, and unlike Arthur, most of them have little hesitation about converting their plots into reality. As Bruhl observes in the opening scene of *Deathtrap:*

> They say that committing murder on paper siphons off the hostile impulses, and I'm sure it does. At the same time though, it opens one to the idea of committing real murder, gives it the familiar feel of a possibility worth considering—just as owning a weapon, and handling it *(Takes an ornate dagger from its place.)* opens one, however slightly, to the idea of using it. *(Toys with dagger, hefts it.)*[14]

In Anthony Shaffer's *Sleuth* (1970), the first major success in the new style of subversive thrillers, and in Nick Hall's *Dead Wrong* (1982), the protagonist is an author of mystery stories who decides to use his skills to get rid of his wife's lover. In Shaffer's play, the writer, Andrew, has invited Milo to his home. He reveals he knows Milo is his wife's lover, but claims he is tired of her and proposes a deal. If Milo will stage a theft of jewelry from the house, he can sell the jewelry abroad and live there with Marguerite, while Andrew pockets the insurance money and pursues his own amours. Milo agrees, and the two set up a rather foolishly elaborate burglary. At its end, however, Andrew draws a gun on Milo and announces that the whole plan was a set-up to allow him to shoot Milo as a house-breaker and get away with it. The entire plot was, after all, the invention of a professional creator of murder mysteries, as the dialogue regularly confirms. Even as he holds the gun on his victim, Andrew considers the situation from a literary point of view:

> ANDREW: . . . The only question to be decided is where you are to be found. Sprawled over the desk like countless colonels in countless studies? Or propped up in the log basket like a rag doll? Which would you prefer—early Agatha Christie or vintage S. S. Van Dyne?
>
> MILO: For Christ's sake, Andrew, this is not a detective story, this is real life. You are talking of doing a real murder. Of killing a real man—don't you understand?[15]

Such comments might serve to warn the audience that the games of reality and illusion being played here are more complex than they might seem, but Andrew has been shown from the beginning to be immersed in his world of mystery fictionality, and generic metacomments of this sort (and the act contains a number of them) are doubtless coded as nothing more than somewhat extreme examples of the comedic self-reflexivity common to this genre. Only as the play progresses do we come to realize how deeply *both* characters are committed to theatricalized action. Milo, not dead, comes back to exact an equivalent revenge on his tormentor, and though not a professional writer of mysteries like Andrew, he proves even more adept at the ludic manipulation of reality they involve. Perhaps this is in part because he is not trapped inside such games, as Andrew seems to be, and has an outsider's understanding of their hollow artificiality. Near the end of the play he challenges his adversary:

> Take a look at yourself, Andrew, and ask yourself a few simple questions about your attachment to the English detective story. Perhaps you might come to realize that the only world you can inhabit is a dead world—a country house world where peers and colonels die in their studies; where butlers steal the port, and pert parlourmaids cringe, weeping, behind green baize doors. It's a world of coldness and class hatred, and two-dimensional characters who are not expected to communicate; it's a world where only the amateurs ever win, and where to be a foreigner is to be automatically a figure of fun. To be puzzled is all.[16]

Craig, the vengeful husband in *Dead Wrong*, is not, like Andrew, a successful writer, but his unpublished thrillers are described by his wife Peggy as "very intricate, very devious . . . perfect murder things with alibis and getting rid of the body."[17] Now Craig confronts Peggy's lover, Allen, and threatens to use the plot of one such manuscript to get rid of him. He has planted cocaine in Allen's apartment and informed the police. Now he gives Allen money and tells him to leave the area. After Allen goes, he remarks "You stupid stud, that's how you dispose of a body—first—then you commit the murder."[18] He then simulates the sounds of a struggle and murder to conclude the scene.

Although *Dead Wrong* offers a premise very similar to that of *Sleuth*, including the staged murder (which very likely will remind followers of the genre of the earlier play), the gimmick is developed quite differently. In *Sleuth*, we thought the murder was real and do not learn the truth until later. Here we know the murder is false, but we do not know the purpose of this staging until later, when Craig begins to torture his wife with the belief he has murdered Allen and hidden his body in the basement. When at last Allen returns, Peggy, driven to distraction by Craig's plot, shoots him thinking he is her husband. In the final turn of the plot, a police inspector, unusually prescient for an officer in a comedy thriller, intuits what has actually happened and arrests Craig for the murder. Justice, if not truth, is served.

Even more complex in their considerations of the interplay between fiction and real dramatic actions are certain comedy thrillers whose author-protagonists are involved both with the conversion of what seems to be reality into fiction, as in *Ask Me No Questions* and *Guilty Conscience*, and the conversion of fiction into what seems to be reality, as in *Sleuth* and *Dead Wrong*. Particularly striking examples of this unstable dynamic are provided by Walter and Peter Marks's *The Butler Did It*, Greenwood and King's *Murder by the Book* and Ira Levin's *Deathtrap*, which, along with *Sleuth*, is among the best-known examples of this genre, as well as one of the most ingeniously self-reflexive.

In *Murder by the Book*, Imogen, an actress, seemingly murders her mystery writing husband, Selwyn, in the middle of the first act, but he returns to life for the surprising first act curtain and later explains that he discovered her plot and put blanks in her gun. He also reveals that he has left a poisoned drink for her at her house so that she would be thought to have died in remorse for having shot him. This whole plot, he suggests, "I conceived . . . as though it were my latest thriller. I even typed out a synopsis."[19] As they laugh together, he reveals that he has, in fact, just poisoned her. In the next scene, having carried Imogen's dead body into the bedroom, Selwyn explains to his secretary and an inquisitive neighbor that she committed suicide in remorse. They have, however, obtained a copy of his synopsis and upset his plot by substituting harmless pills for his poison. Imogen, who has feigned death, returns unharmed. Selwyn, unshaken, claims that the entire evening has been a hoax from start to finish, with his secretary and the neighbor as victims, to provide "authentic reactions" for his fiction. Much in the manner of the author in *Ask Me No Questions*, Selwyn exults:

> All my life I've been striving for the perfect meld of fact and fiction. They say I can write ingenious stories which entertain the reader without ever convincing him they could really happen. Well, now I shall create a masterpiece about this evening with the knowledge that everything in it could, should, and did happen.[20]

Neither author nor public can so readily accept such a return to stability in the fictive world of the modern comedy thriller, however. To test his story, the victims suggest Selwyn take the pills originally intended for Imogen. Since he appears willing to do so, they believe his story and do not insist. When they leave, Imogen congratulates Selwyn for so brilliant a lie to cover the real murder attempt. Selwyn responds that it was not a lie. The whole thing was a hoax, on Imogen as well. She proposes a toast and slips in the pills to find out the truth. She will know, but we never shall, since the curtain falls as she tells Selwyn what she has done. As is often the case in comedy thrillers, we are never in any doubt about who done it, but we are quite unsure about what has been done, or upon what level of fiction or reality it has been done. In terms of the dramatic action, what is Selwyn, really—a murderer or a mystery author? Have we been witnessing reality (the honest psychological reactions of those being manipulated) being utilized in the service of fiction

(Selwyn's planned story) or fiction (the proposed story) being utilized in the service of reality (an actual attempted murder)? The play is constructed to suggest first one possibility, then the other and, ultimately, to provide us with no secure interpretation.

Less complex, but perhaps even more disturbing in terms of generic expectations, is the situation of Clifford Jordan in Francis Durbridge's *Deadly Nightcap* (1986). Clifford enters the play in a highly conventional fashion, examining witnesses and suspects after the murder of Jack, which he does in a highly competent fashion. During the second act, however, one of the suspects congratulates him on his recent book, in which he has taken several famous unsolved murder cases and presented "possible explanations" of them. "Have you ever thought of leaving the police and becoming a full-time writer?" he is asked, to which he replies "I think of nothing else, Mrs. Warren."[21] This would be an odd interchange in any case, but is especialy so in a modern thriller, where the writer, as the subverter of authority and order, is almost invariably opposed to the detective.

Jack's murder is not solved, and, six months later, Clifford, now a successful author, has left the force and is going to America to promote his work. He has continued to see Jack's wife, Sarah, and he brings her some notes he has made about the events surrounding Jack's death. "I did my best to look at the sequence of events in a completely detached, analytical way," he explains, "as if I was devising another chapter of the book."[22] He gives the notes to Sarah to read, promising that when she has done so, they will be destroyed and forgotten. As Sarah reads, we see Clifford's scenario enacted. Jack's mistress, Anna, urged by him to aid in a murder plot against Sarah, refuses at the last moment to do so, and when Jack turns on her, she kills him in self-defense. Sarah agrees to shield her. Having read this reconstruction, Sarah admits to Clifford that he has guessed the truth, but true to his promise, he destroys the notes and she promises to come with him to America. The murder remains officially unsolved, a "perfect crime" against a husband by a wife and her writer-lover, carried out, in a sense, retrospectively. Clifford's decision to leave the role of detective for that of writer proves, at the end, to have indeed been a move from relation to truth and fictionality that each character traditionally represents.

The field of play between the reality of murder and its fictionalization is also the real subject of Ira Levin's *Deathtrap*. Its opening situation, as has been noted, suggests that of Watkin's *Not in the Book* (1958), where a young mystery writer brings his first effort to an older man for advice and encouragement. In Levin's play, the situation is much more closely tied to the world of thriller writing itself. In Watkin's play, the older man, a respectable businessman, sees, in the plot brought to him, a way to get rid of a blackmailer. In Levin's play, the older man is himself a mystery playwright, now in a discouraging dry spell, and instead of using the young author's plot as a murder scheme, he jokes with his wife about taking over the plot to restore his flagging reputation and murdering the young man to cover his theft.

When the young writer comes to visit, Sidney's wife, Myra, watches in mounting horror as he seems to be ready to carry out this plan. After Sidney tricks Clifford into putting on a pair of handcuffs, even the young author begins to sense the situation, which he suggests has the makings of a good thriller:

> ". . . a young playwright sends his first play to an older playwright who conducted a seminar that the young playwright attended. Nobody else has read it, and then he comes to *visit* the older playwright, *to get some ideas for rewrites* . . . and the older playwright would have nothing much going for him at the time . . .
> SIDNEY: An enormous concatenation of unlikely circumstances, don't you think?[23]

In fact, the threatened murder is apparently carried out and the unfortunate Clifford presumably buried in the garden. In the next scene, however, as Sidney glories in his good fortune, the "corpse" returns and attacks him. We then discover that all this was staged by Sidney and Clifford, who are in fact lovers, in a successful plot to stimulate a fatal heart attack in Myra, a situation recalling the classic French suspense film *Diabolique*.

In the second act, the murderers have apparently gotten away with their crime and have settled down together as writer and secretary, Sidney still unable to think of new plots but Clifford working rapidly on what he claims is a story about life in a welfare office. Becoming suspicious, Sidney sneaks a look at this manuscript and begins to read, repeating, in horror, his opening line: "Deathtrap. A thriller in two acts." He goes on to read the stage directions: ". . . a handsomely converted stable grafted onto an authentic Colonial house. Sliding doors upstage center . . ." and so on, in exactly the words we can read in the printed version or see realized on stage.[24] At the opening, however, there was no such play, but now one seems to be in process, and it is in fact the play we have just seen. Clifford, confronted, is happy to confirm this, recounting the events in his play, which precisely follow those of act one of the *Deathtrap* we have been watching. Sidney, perhaps recalling the plot of *Write Me a Murder*, sees Clifford's project as the prelude to prison for them both, but when he is unable to convince Clifford to give it up, he agrees to help him with the second act, which is giving Clifford trouble.

This is, however, only a ruse. Pretending to work out physical details in the new act, Sidney scuffles with Clifford, then pulls a gun on him. As the inevitable theatrical storm rages outside he explains: "*Deathtrap* is over. We're now into theatre *vérité*." Rather than let Clifford finish the play, he must actually kill him. But when he fires, he finds that Clifford, anticipating him, has replaced the bullets with blanks. Now Clifford pulls his own gun and reverses the roles, with the reflexive observation: "Sit *down. Peripetia?* Reversal? You talked about it the first day of the seminar. Important element of all drama."[25] Once again Clifford has tricked Sidney into giving him material. What they have done since the beginning of this act, from the discovery of the self-referential manuscript to the recent peripetia, has provided him with his second act. Only the conclusion remains, and Clifford suggests he will let Sidney's plan work out, the older writer will shoot the younger, but then confess his crime and kill himself.

Bert States has described the theatre as "the medium, par excellence, that consumes the real in its realist forms" and, indeed, has argued that the progressive encroachment of the theatre upon reality is necessary for the continuing nourishment of the illusionary system.[26] Occasionally in the modern drama, this dynamic has been foregrounded by the device of making a character in the play (like Trigorin in Chekhov's *The Sea Gull*) convert the "real lives" of those around him into theatre. *Deathtrap* is driven by a particularly extended development of this device, so that the "reality" of the stage world we are watching is continually, act by act, being "consumed" by the fictionalization of this reality into a mystery thriller, presumably the very mystery thriller we are watching. Not even the deaths of the two creators of this self-devouring machine can stop it, since the survivors also see the possibilities of a highly profitable stage play in what has happened, and the play ends as they fall into what seems likely to become yet another murderous argument over who will control this valuable property.

A very similar point is made by the overall action of *The Butler Did It*, in which an author/director attempts to use material of real life to improve his whodunnit, then attempts to use material from the whodunnit to carry out a real murder, and finally, when the plot backfires on himself, seeks to convert his own death into a publicity stunt that will insure the success of his play. The interpenetration of "reality" and "fiction" is continually stressed, even in the selection of the murder weapon, which is a book with poisoned pages in the manner of the Medici. Not only is this literally "murder by the book," but the book itself contributes to the play of fictionalization and parodic reference, as the author, Tony, explains:

> A curious murder weapon—"The Way of All Flesh" by Samuel Butler. Yes. It was the murderer's private joke. The Butler did it![27]

The complex self-referential structure of plays like *Deathtrap* or *The Butler Did It* makes clear some of the difficulties of this genre. For all its apparent freewheeling play with traditional codes, strategies, and expectations, the modern comedy thriller presents to its authors a challenge not greatly different from that of the more traditional detective drama. As Clifford in *Deathtrap* observes: "It's a tradition: a superbly challenging theatrical framework in which every possible variation seems to have been played. Can I conjure up a few new ones? Can I startle an audience that's *been* on Angel Street, that's dialed "M" for murder, that's witnessed the prosecution . . ."[28]

This is indeed the basic challenge, not only for traditional detective fiction authors, but also for the authors of postmodern thrillers. The game has changed from hiding clues and tricking expectations about the identity of the murderer to finding new ways to trick expectations of a more basic type, from finding new ways of committing murder to finding new ways of keeping the audience unsure whether murder has been committed or not, from finding new tricks within the rules to finding new tricks that will expose the rules for audiences increasingly prepared for such tricks. There is a natural trend toward more complex and more radical subversions as audiences for this subgenre become more difficult to surprise, and this is surely why, during the 1980s, a number of such plays turned from the sort of playing with the fictional process in general that we see in *Deathtrap* or *Not in the Book* to dismantling the phenomenological processes of the theatrical medium itself.

5 DEAD WRONG

> "Of course, if we were doing a thriller, you could drink the Sanka, die, and come back in the next scene."
>
> —Tony in *The Butler Did It*

If one were to attempt to find a single narrative element that would be common to every example of the comedy thriller, that element would have to be murder, a preoccupation which this subgenre shares with the earlier forms upon which it is based. Theft, kidnapping, sabotage, and other crimes have served as bases for mystery dramas, but in these, as in detective fiction as a whole, the vast majority of narratives are built upon the commission of a murder. Murder is the universal subject of the modern comedy thrillers.

Stoppard's *The Real Inspector Hound* acknowledges the importance of this "given" by opening with a man's body sprawled in front of a large settee in the drawing room of Muldoon Manor. The critic, Birdboot, arriving to review the show, inquires of the senior critic, Moon, already arrived:

> . . . it's a sort of *thriller*, isn't it?
> MOON: Is it?

BIRDBOOT: That's what I heard. Who-killed thing?—nobody-will-leave-the-house?
MOON: I suppose so. Underneath.
BIRDBOOT: *Underneath?!* It's a whodunnit, man!—Look at it! *They look at it. The room. The body. Silence.*[1]

As this parody suggests, the dead body in the drawing room is an unmistakable sign of the detective thriller. As Haugen observed, the audience can "breathe easier again, sit back and relax" once the lights come on to expose a body, since they now know that "the show is on."[2] The dead body provides the central concern for the ensuing action, and its appearance is the initiating incident for the whole traditional machinery of the police inquiries, the search for clues, the testing of alibis, and, eventually, the unmasking of the murderer. The operation of this machinery is also parodied by Stoppard, who, having foregrounded the convention of the body in the drawing room, proceeds in equally extreme fashion to flout the expected consequences of this. As the act proceeds, the other characters wander in and out of the room, never noticing the obvious corpse, until near the end of the first act when Inspector Hound suddenly notices he is standing on the body and calls the attention of the others to it.

Since the goal of the modern comedy thriller drama is to provide a series of shocks and surprises, often by epistemological shifts or the radical disruption of accepted codes, it is hardly surprising that the murder and the appearance of the body, as a central element of the traditional mystery, now becomes a central site for the introduction of narrative and epistemological instability. The dramatic cozy represents a relatively straightforward world, the stability and rationality of which is disrupted by a murder and restored when one of the group of characters presented to us is eventually unmasked as the murderer. In the permanently unstable and self-consciously theatrical world of the comedy thriller, murders often occur, perhaps more often per play than in the cozies, but the audience can rarely be sure how the murders are to be interpreted. Almost never is the question the traditional, "who is the murderer?" It may well be, "who has been murdered?" or "has the murder really oc-curred?" even (or perhaps especially) when we have seen it with our own eyes.

Introducing confusion over who has been murdered would seem a provocative reversal of the traditional concern of detec-tive dramas, but this device has not often been used, surely because of the technical difficulties in maintaining a mystery about the identity of a body in the very small world of a dramatic cast of characters. *The Real Inspector Hound* provides one of the most surprising of all identifications of dead bodies. The body lies onstage from the beginning and is perfectly obvious to, but generally ignored by, the other characters who carry on the usual activities of such a drama, accompanied by the comments of two reviewers in the audience, the regular, Birdboot, and Moon, a second-stringer who is substituting for his absent col-league, Higgs. Later, as the play develops, Birdboot is literally drawn into it by his attraction to the female characters. Left alone on stage at one point, he finally examines the body more closely. To his horror, he discovers that it is Higgs! In a sense, Stoppard has carefully prepared for this astonishing moment, both by noting the absence of Higgs at the beginning and by demonstrating, through Birdboot, that "real-world" people can enter this thriller. Nevertheless, the coding of the body as part of the thriller, indeed, as has already been noted, as one of its most reliable indices, is so strong that the identification of Higgs is even more of a shock than Birdboot's original invasion of the stage space. Moreover, since "Higgs" never appears as a living being in either the "real" world of the critics or the "fictive" world of Muldoon Manor, he does not have to be identified in the program, and so the audience has not a hint of who the mysterious body may turn out to be.

In a more conventional plot, where the victim has to be se-lected from among a fairly small group of known and identified characters who inhabit a single, circumscribed, fictive world, this sort of trickery is, of course, not possible. Still, suspense about the identity of the victim has been occasionally utilized. Alec Coppel's *The Gazebo* (1958) is one of the few effective examples of this. A mystery writer whose wife is being blackmailed invites the blackmailer to his home, shoots him, and buries the body under the foundations of a new gazebo being erected in his back yard. Soon after, a police officer arrives, checking the names on a list of people found in the blackmailer's apartment where the blackmailer has just been discovered, shot. Although we still are, of course, concerned here with who actually killed the blackmailer, we are much more concerned, as is the protagonist, with who he has actually shot and buried under the gazebo. The solution to both questions eventually involves bringing in several more characters and a police-gangster plot quite out of harmony with the concerns of later thrillers.

Among these, only a few use the device of misleading the audience about the victim. In Anthony Shaffer's *Murderer*, the protagonist, Norman, has for some time sought the occasion to murder his wife, Elizabeth, and we apparently see this happen at the beginning of the second act. Elizabeth is dimly seen and heard behind the translucent bathroom door. Norman hesitates outside the door then:

> . . . *with sudden resolve he cautiously opens the bathroom door to its full extent. We see him approach the bath-capped head almost overtopped by bubbles, and through the swirling clouds of steam we watch the whole murder—the head pushed under, the wildly threshing legs—the water slopped over in the struggle, and then after an appreciable time, the cessation of all movement.*[3]

A very effective and amusing suspense scene follows when a police inspector calls and wishes to use the bathroom. Scarcely is he safely out of the way than Norman is staggered to see his wife, perfectly healthy, return from a trip. Many in the audience doubtless share his immediate shock, but the tension this creates about the body in the bath cannot be maintained, as it is in *Gazebo* with its much larger cast, typical of the 1950s. The program for *Murderer* lists only the inspector; Norman; Elizabeth, his wife; and Milly, his lover; so even though it is several more pages before Milly is revealed as his victim, the audience can have little doubt about who she is.

A much more elaborate trick is played with the murder victim in Francis Durbridge's *Deadly Nightcap*. At the end of the first scene, the ruthless protagonist, Jack, shoots his brother-in-law and business partner, who has become suspicious of Jack's shady dealings in the company, and arranges the death to appear a suicide. Jack then embarks on an elaborate plot to convince everyone that his wife, Sarah, has become depressed and psychologically unstable because of this suicide, so that he can kill her in turn. In typical comedy thriller fashion, he organizes a murder scheme with the aid of another woman, though the general construction of the action continually suggests another thriller tradition rarely utilized in comedy thrillers, what might be called (borrowing a term from mystery novels) a woman-in-jeopardy plot. Some of the great thriller classics, such as *Angel Street* (1938), *Kind Lady* (1935), or Ira Levin's more recent *Veronica's Room* (1974), create their primary suspense not from a murder intrigue, but from the victimization of a vulnerable woman, usually by a husband or others who cut her off from the rest of the world by claiming that she is insane. In *Deadly Nightcap* this familiar situation is developed not to provide suspense for an entire play, but to provide it for most of the first act and, more importantly, to set up a major subversion of this convention at the act's conclusion. The penultimate scene of this act ends with Jack's scheme headed for apparent success. Sarah has drunk the drugged contents from the glass he has given her and has fallen unconscious, and as the curtain falls, Jack is preparing to carry her to the pool where she will be found drowned. At this point we seem to have turned from the "woman-in-jeopardy" plot back to a more traditional detective drama. The following scene

opens the next morning in traditional fashion with a police inspector interviewing the housekeeper, who has found the body
in the pool. Next, Geoffrey, a former employee of Jack, arrives
and insists that Sarah would not have committed suicide but
must have been murdered. The inspector encourages him to
elaborate on this idea, but as he is doing so, the presumed victim, Sarah, walks in. Sarah and the inspector then reveal to the
stunned Geoffrey (and the stunned audience) that Jack was the
one found in the pool that morning, murdered. The effect of
this powerful coup de théâtre comes from a subversion of two
of the most basic actant roles in the mystery genre, those of
murderer and victim. Jack, actually committing murder in the
first scene and participating in all the plotting activity in subsequent scenes, has been established, from the beginning, as the
murderer, while his wife, with a strong assist from the conventions of "jeopardy" plots, has been consistently portrayed as the
victim. Even the usual codifications of the comedy thriller are
challenged by this, by now traditional, double frustration of
narrative and generic expectations.

Even after the murder of Jack is revealed and *Deadly Nightcap*
continues with a generally conventional examination of witnesses and suspects, the unpredictable Sarah continues to confuse the plot with false confessions. She first provides to
Inspecting Superintendent Jordan an elaborate but false description of how she killed her husband, and later, after Geoffrey
dies quite naturally of a heart attack, tries to implicate herself
in that death as well. In each case she gives a convincing and
detailed description that Jordan subsequently refutes with contradictory evidence. Her motivation for these fantasies is not
clear until the final scene, but in the meantime, they provide
alternate and destabilizing versions of the "reality" of both of
these deaths.

Rather than play with the traditional question of "who did it"
or its less flexible mirror image of "who was it done to," modern
thriller writers have overwhelmingly favored the introduction of

instability into the murder act itself, asking many variations of the question, "did it in fact happen?" Since the entire action of the mystery drama is grounded on this event, calling its reality into question in effect calls into question the purpose and the operation of the entire generic structure. The easiest but, theatrically, least effective domain for the placement of murders that may or may not have happened is, of course, off-stage, as detailed in the narratives of the dramatic characters, as we see in *Deadly Nightcap*. Approximately one in every three modern thrillers contains one or more accounts of a murder off-stage. Probably the most familiar example of this device is the report by Milo that he has killed Andrew's mistress, Téa, framed him for the crime, and alerted the police, a story that stimulates much of what occurs in the second act of *Sleuth*. A similar trick is central to *The Business of Murder*, which cleverly turns the dynamics of the normal thriller inside-out by having an outsider, a convicted criminal with a grudge, utilize the traditional triangle for his own revenge scheme by telling a police officer and his lover, a writer of mysteries, that he has killed the officer's wife and framed the lovers for the crime. In these cases, as in most such cases, the murders have not in fact happened and are known by their narrators not to have happened, but they are presented in such a way as to convince one or more of the characters of their reality, often with corroborating evidence. The audience, especially if they have seen several works in this genre, is likely to be more suspicious, but since "real" deaths also occur in such plays and expectations are routinely thwarted, they are forced always to keep open at least the possibility that such reports are true.

Those thrillers that take place on several levels of "reality"—set partly in the protagonist's mind or revealed at some point in their action as theatrical rehearsals or performances—almost invariably relate the false death to a shift in level. At least the first "murder" in *Guilty Conscience* is designed to mislead the audience, until they realize that this, and much of what they will subsequently witness, takes place in the imagination of the protagonist. Similarly, the murders in *Out of Sight—Out of Murder* take place in the fantasy world created by Peter with characters from conventional fiction, and he can "cancel" these murders by simply typing "The End" on his manuscript. The resurrection of Mrs. Butler and the arrival on stage of the director in *The Butler Did It* utilizes the trick of shifting the situation from "reality" to "stage fiction" in a manner reminiscent of Pirandello's *Tonight We Improvise* (1930), where a death scene is played with apparent belief and sincerity by all parties, but is then exposed as fiction by the appearance of the director commenting upon the actors' achievement. In each of these plays, deaths, on one level of "reality" or in one "fictive universe," disappear when consideration moves to another, exposing them as fictional devices. The acknowledgment of the embedding of the comedy thriller in the process of imagination or theatricalization is obviously a particularly appropriate means of destabilizing the murder trope, but one may also see this strategy as a specific example of a more general strategy, which is to emphasize the constructedness and artificiality of the murder by placing it more generally in the realm of imagination and fantasy.

More common, and certainly more theatrical than reported deaths, are the deaths in comedy thrillers that are actually witnessed by the audience. Again and again in these plays, we find characters apparently murdered, often in bloody detail, following all the normal "death" codifications of the stage—guns fired, knives thrust into bodies, agonized cries, senseless bodies, and splattered brains and gore.

When such "murders" occur in the middle of an act or scene, the "murdered" characters often subvert this codification immediately by springing back to "life" (the gun was loaded with blanks, the dagger has a retractable blade). Since in fact blanks and retractable blades are traditional means for "real" murders to be shown on stage, the introduction of them into the narrative "reality" of the thriller almost invariably introduces at some level, a consciousness of theatricality, a consciousness that may well be specifically emphasized, as it is in Simon Gray's *Stage Struck*. The loaded gun is introduced early in the first act, and Robert, inspecting it, immediately places it in a theatrical context:

> Yes, live all right, like old times, the number of Agatha Christies and so forth I've had to handle these in, or had them pointed at me and been shot at or killed by, with blanks of course *(he laughs)* or kept them loaded up for the last scene of *Hedda Gabler,* three different productions and in two of them I longed for live ammunition, given the ladies in question.[4]

In the second act, Robert draws a gun upon his wife's psychoanalyst, Widdecombe, fires a bullet into a dummy to show him that it is loaded, and threatens to kill him. Once again Robert foregrounds the theatricalized nature of the situation:

> ROBERT: . . . Sit down. *(Widdecombe goes to sit down)* No, not there. The sight-lines are terrible. *(Widdecombe moves to another chair)* Nor there—you'd be upstaging me. Now bring that chair over . . . *(Widdecombe follows Robert's instructions)*—that's right. And put it there. I could make a good props man out of you, Widdecombe, if I didn't need you for a leading part.[5]

After a fairly lengthy sequence of tormenting the unfortunate Widdecombe, the scene appears to approach a climax. Robert counts "one . . . two . . . three . . ." as Widdecombe cries "No no no no." Then:

> *(They stare at each other for a second. Robert shoots him in the stomach. Widdecombe screams, lurches back, clutching at stomach, stops)*
> ROBERT: That last bit was rather good. No notes at all there. *(Widdecombe collapses into a chair. Robert tosses the gun into Widdecombe's lap)* You're still grasping the first stage of my plan, are you? *(He crosses to the telephone, talks as he dials)* It's to give you, you see, a vivid taste of death. A glimpse over the abyss. A spasm of eternity. And so forth. So that you'd learn something about the irrationality of the human psyche.[6]

The effect of such a sequence within an act, when the false death is immediately exposed, is not only to disrupt a conventional situation and arrangement of action (the normal dramatic build is undercut at the moment it reaches its climax), but also, as this example in particular illustrates, to stress its theatrical calculation.

Deaths placed at or near the ends of acts or scenes are just as likely to be eventually exposed as false, but their generic subversion works in a more extended and elaborate manner. First, and most importantly, their placement within the dramatic structure and their presentation to us as "real" murders make them indistinguishable narratologically from traditional deaths in normal detective drama. There is thus a strong narrative "pull" toward this "normal" reading, countered, of course, for audience members who have seen a number of modern comedy thrillers, by a recognition that in plays of this type such "murders" are frequently tricks. This very doubleness of possible interpretation sets up a particular kind of tension, especially in more recent examples of this genre.

Sleuth and *Deathtrap*, the most praised of the modern comedy thrillers, provide two of the most striking uses of this sort of false death and, in their different strategies, also suggest something of the changes in this subgenre over a decade. Despite all the hints of disguise, theatricality, and fictionalization, Andrew's shooting of Milo at the end of the first act of *Sleuth* is clearly meant to be taken, and for most of its original audience members surely was taken, as a real murder within the fictive world of the play. It conformed both to the general codes of realistic drama (the determination and motive of Andrew, the fear and pleading of Milo, the long build-up to the moment, and the shooting itself, where the gun is seen and heard to fire and Milo falls down the stairs and lies motionless at their foot) and, more importantly, to the codes of mystery play, according to which a cleverly plotted murder is committed in its proper place at the end of the first act, and the audience can now look forward to the arrival of the detective, at the beginning of the next act, who will match wits with and eventually expose the murderer.

The opening of the second act, however, thwarted any such normal generic expectations. The curtain rises on the same room, surely sometime later, but with no investigating detective present and no signs of the previous action. Andrew is chatting on the telephone, his life apparently back on its normal course. Have the police come and gone? If so, why have we been deprived of the necessary next step in a mystery drama—their questions about the death? If not, where is the body, and why has the room been returned to normal? The confusion is increased a few moments later when Inspector Doppler arrives and begins questioning Andrew about Milo, who has disappeared. What is happening seems impossible to reconcile, narratively, with what was shown in the previous act.

Finally, under pressure from the inspector, Andrew provides an explanation for these seemingly irreconcilable developments. Andrew did not wish to kill, but only to frighten and humiliate, his rival. The shot directed at Milo was a blank, and Milo did not die, but fainted from the shock. After recovering, he left the house and Andrew has not seen him since. This explanation clarifies the odd opening of the second act, but scarcely is it advanced before it also is called into question. The Inspector finds blood on the banister and rug and Milo's clothing hidden at the back of a wardrobe, evidence incompatible with Andrew's story. Again, instability is introduced. Did we see a murder at the end of the first act or not?

Today, after two decades of other plays playing similar tricks with generic expectations and the stability of the fictive world of mystery drama, audiences for such plays have learned to accept, and even to expect, the sort of tricks played in *Sleuth*, but in 1970, despite the popularity of the play, its subversion of expectations stimulated some controversy. In his review for the *New York Times*, Walter Kerr characterized the play as basically "a teaser for the buffs" and predicted that he would "hear detective story loyalists arguing from now until Christmas whether all is or is not cricket on the Music Box stage."[7] Strictly speaking, *Sleuth* sets itself, from the beginning, against the traditional "fair-play rule" articulated by Dorothy Sayers, since the audience sees a plot set up that is purportedly designed to mislead the police. On the other hand, variations of this device, as we have seen, have been accepted in the "howdunnits" for some time, and it is most unlikely, had *Sleuth* continued along the lines of, for example, Milne's *The Perfect Alibi*, that even a conservative critic like Martin Gottfried would have had any serious objections to it.

It was, however, precisely the manipulation of the material dealing with the false death that Gottfried, saying quite correctly that the play concealed essential information from the audience in order to sow its confusion, found particularly objectionable in *Sleuth*. Clearly, had Shaffer kept the curtain up a few moments longer at the end of his first act, this dilemma would be resolved, but that, of course, is exactly the point. To condemn him for not doing so, or for arbitrarily setting up an ambiguous situation in this way, would be like condemning Agatha Christie, or charging her for arbitrary ambiguity, for having the lights go out in *The Mousetrap* just before the murderer strikes, since if they stay on, we would know who the murderer is. What Gottfried does not see is that the device used in *The Mousetrap* and *Sleuth* is, in fact, the same, but the focus of the genre itself has shifted. In Christie, we are still concerned with the traditional question of the identity of the murderer. In Shaffer, we are no longer asking "whodunnit?" or even "how was it done?" but, in fact, "was it done at all?" The very basis of the reality of the dramatic action is here called into question, and Shaffer has withheld the information that would give an epistemological grounding to his action, just as Christie has withheld the information that would reveal her murderer.

Deathtrap, less than a decade later, already faces the problem of finding new ways to surprise and destabilize audience readings and expectations, given that these audiences (as the young playwright, Clifford, in the play complains) have very likely seen *Sleuth* and a number of similar works. Much more effort is expended in *Deathtrap* to convince the audience that they are seeing a "real" death. Instead of the very modest (and in fact ambiguous) stage directions dealing with this matter in *Sleuth:*

> ANDREW *pulls the trigger.* MILO *falls backwards down the stairs and lies still.* ANDREW, *satisfied that he has done his work well, smiles to himself.*[8]

Deathtrap describes the "murder" of Clifford in brutal detail, of which the following is a representative sample:

> SIDNEY *hauls* CLIFFORD *about by the garrotte, evading his groping hands, his kicking legs. A lamp falls.* CLIFFORD *catches one of* SIDNEY'S *hands and wrenches at it. Blood trickles down* CLIFFORD'S *wire-bound throat.* MYRA *turns and looks and turns away again, never stopping her moaning and lamentation.* CLIFFORD, *pop-eyed and hawking, falls forward before the fireplace, his shackled arms outflung;* SIDNEY *goes down with him, keeping his fierce hold on the handles.*

This grisly sequence ends with the sort of statement that was pointedly NOT made in the stage directions of *Sleuth:* "*When* CLIFFORD *is finally and surely dead,* SIDNEY *relaxes his grip.*"[9]

The graphic brutality of *Deathtrap* seeks to convince the audience that no misunderstanding is possible here, that Clifford is indeed "finally and surely dead." Nor does the ensuing scene, as in *Sleuth*, suggest any ambiguity about this. Sidney returns from burying the body, brushing dirt from his clothing and begins planning the marketing of his dead victim's play. Clifford's return, a few pages later, is sudden, unexpected, and violent. He bursts into the room, covered with dirt and his throat still bleeding, wielding a piece of firewood that he smashes down again and again on Sidney's head. When Sidney collapses and lies still, Clifford advances on Myra, who is shrieking and cowering in horror. As he raises the firewood, she collapses. He bends over her, checks her wrist, and announces, "She's dead. I'm positive," and adds, as Sidney joins him, "it worked." We find that both "deaths" have been staged by Clifford and Sidney to induce a real one—an attack of Myra's weak heart.

Clifford, like Milo, has returned in "disguise," though not as a new character, but as Sidney's victim. The stunned audience, like Myra, naturally assumes that Sidney, in error, buried Clifford still alive and that Clifford has returned to seek revenge. The suddenness, unexpectedness, and brutal physicality of the attack scarcely leaves them time to wonder if this might be some trick. As soon as the trick has had its effect on Myra, and the audience, it is explained. The strategy of this "perfect murder" is strongly reminiscent of Henri-Georges Clouzot's classic horror film *Diabolique*, where the return of a man from "death" is also a carefully planned hoax to induce a fatal heart attack in his wife. The shocking "return from death" is found in a number of comedy thrillers, often consciously or unconsciously echoing Clouzot's film (as when the presumably dead Gus emerges dripping from the jacuzzi in *Fatal Attraction*, just as Clouzot's husband emerges from the bath). None of them, however, utilize the particular suspense strategy of the film, which constantly suggests that something supernatural may be going on, since spectators of detective thrillers, long accustomed to faked deaths, would surely interpret any hint of a character's continued presence as a trick of this sort, thus diminishing both surprise and suspense. Once the trick has been played, it can be quickly acknowledged, and the action can move on to new complications.

The convention of the false death is so well established in comedy thrillers by the late 1970s that it can serve as a source of parodic humor in David Fulk's *The Potman Spoke Sooth*, which features several scenes of general extermination, followed by a brief pause, after which everyone gets back up, with one excuse or another, to explain why they are still alive and to continue with the play.[10] The establishment of the false death convention means also that it can begin to be used as a new locus of destabilization within this genre. Already in Francis Durbridge's *Suddenly at Home* (1973), we can see this process at work. In the first scene, Glenn sets up a murder plot against his wife Maggie with the aid of his mistress, Sheila. Near the end of the next scene, Glenn suffocates Maggie on stage—a murder carefully detailed in the stage directions—and the following scene shows their plot working out as planned, until a surprising phone call arrives from Sam, a former lover of Maggie's they were hoping to frame for the murder. Sam has called to inform them that Maggie, thought missing, has safely arrived at his house. Left alone, the conspirators voice their confusion:

> SHEILA: But what's happened? Where is Maggie?
> GLENN: You know damn well where she is!
> SHEILA: Then why did Sam say she was at the cottage?
> GLENN: *(tensely, obviously worried)* I don't know! I just don't know!
> SHEILA: *(after a pause, softly)* Glenn, are you sure about Maggie? You didn't make a mistake?
> GLENN: Of course I didn't make a mistake! *(In spite of his denial it is obvious that the same incredible thought has occurred to him)*[11]

The same "incredible thought" will obviously occur to a modern thriller audience, and it is a mark of the subversion of traditional codes that has already occurred that an audience is more likely to disbelieve in the very graphic death that they have actually witnessed, than in the possibility that Maggie is truly dead and that Sam, for some reason, is lying. In fact, *Suddenly at Home* relies precisely upon this unlikely reception situation to play its next trick, since it is soon revealed that Maggie is in fact dead and Sam, for reasons not yet explained in the play, *is* lying. Scarcely has the "false death" been encoded into the practice of thriller mystification than it is available for this sort of destabilization.

In *The Butler Did It*, a more openly self-conscious contribution to the genre, Tony, the presumed author and director of this play, also appears as a character and, quite correctly, remarks upon the device of the false death as a key distinction between the comedy thriller and the more traditional whodunnit: "Of course, if we were doing a thriller, you could drink the Sanka, die, and come back in the next scene. But since 'The Butler Did It' is a whodunit, you die and stay dead. All right. To work!"[12] Since Tony's own play, *The Butler Did It*, is a whodunnit, the death in it is "real," but since the actual play we are watching, *The Butler Did It*, is a thriller, we should naturally expect it to contain at least one false death. Having already pointed out this expectation, however, the play could not also fulfill the generic expectation of uncertainty and surprise if it simply presented a bloody murder in the manner of *Deathtrap*, which would surely be immediately interpreted by the audience as a trick. Instead, the play openly sets up a trick and then subverts it. As part of the rehearsal process, Tony arranges for Natalie to pretend to really die during one of the rehearsals. Clearly a "Method" director, Tony explains that:

> the only way we're going to make the audience feel is to make the *actors* feel. We have to make the actors react authentically, with the kind of shock and horror they'd experience at seeing a real murder in their own lives.[13]

At rehearsal the next day, Natalie carries off a convincing attack, and in the following scene, Tony, presumably returning from the hospital, reports her death. Her fellow actors accept this fiction, though the audience can enjoy being in on the trick. Scarcely has Tony finished, however, when the situation takes a new turn. A detective arrives to investigate the "death." Tony is staggered; this was not in his scenario. He confesses that he hired two actors to pose as an ambulance team to carry off the "stricken" actress, but the detective reports that soon after, she truly went into convulsions and died. The audience, a party to the "false death" plot, are now placed in the familiar, comedy thriller situation of uncertainty. The question is not, "is Natalie dead," but rather, "on what level of reality, if any, is she dead?"

In vain, Tony tries to explain to the detective that the poison was fake, the murder staged. He is placed under arrest. Then, as his rights are being read to him, we return from the world of "reality" to that of the stage. The lights go out; the characters shout in confusion. Suddenly, a spotlight shines on the window seat, and Natalie pops out, arms raised, emitting a piercing scream. When some measure of calm is restored, this interchange takes place:

> TONY (*To* NATALIE) What the hell are you doing?
> NATALIE: Just what you told me to do . . . come back from the dead and interrupt the investigation.
> TONY: But not as a zombie.
> NATALIE: I know. But when I snuck in and started watching all of you from the wings, playing out our whodunit scene, I thought it needed a little shock effect—like in a thriller.[14]

A clever circularity of convention and commentary has thus been carried out. We are signalled, within the play, about the device of the false death; we see a false death set up, then destabilized; and finally, we are surprised by the very trick we were warned to expect, capped off with a final comment about its centrality in the type of play we are watching.

In order to work its trick, *The Butler Did It* returns to the rather neglected strategy of the falsely reported off-stage death, but this strategy remains an unusual one. Most comedy thrillers prefer the shock and realism of on-stage murders or murder attempts, and because audiences have become accustomed to such murders often turning out to be tricks, these "death" events, in more recent works, have generally been overcoded with as much graphic detail as possible. No longer will a simple gun with blanks and a fainting victim be expected to achieve the effect, as it did in *Sleuth*. Now further authenticating "death" coding is necessary, like the gore in *Deathtrap*, to convince the audience of its "reality." The detective in the parody *The Potman Spoke Sooth* is not fooled when Mrs. Wiggins is discovered on the floor with a meat cleaver in her back, since, as he remarks: "Surely you didn't think me stupid enough not to notice your pulse beat, which you carelessly neglected to terminate."[15] This difficulty has not escaped the attention of others. In *Murder by the Book,* the presumably dead Selwyn's pulse is felt, first by Imogen, who has shot him, and then by the next door neighbor, Peter, and later again by Imogen. After Selwyn's surprising return, he explains that he was wearing a small rubber ball taped over the artery in his armpit so that he could briefly cut off the flow of blood to his wrist whenever he wished.[16] Robert, in *Stage Struck,* bleeds profusely, both at the time of his "death" and later, at his return, when he *"rises up from behind the sofa, shaking, pointing a finger, his eyes upward, as in death, his mouth open. A great spurt of fresh blood pours from his mouth."* Then, having enjoyed the horror of his wife, he wipes away the blood, remarking casually, "Sorry. Couldn't resist using the extra blood capsule. Still, it's what I always say. Certain moments you *can't* go over the top."[17]

Indeed, among such moments are surely those of the fake deaths and resurrections in the thrillers, since only by pushing death codifications to their limits can thriller authors continue to hope that audiences will accept them. If blanks can no longer be relied upon to produce the proper effect, gore may be added, and when gore is too easily read as possible stage blood, more extreme measures still may be employed, as we see in Bernard Slade's *An Act of the Imagination* where a woman is shot and, according to the stage directions, her brains are splattered on the wall behind. Even so extreme an ostentation of the signs of death can no longer be trusted, since soon after this *grand guignol* moment, the "corpse" arises, like Robert in *Stage Struck,* from behind the sofa and participates in the arrest of the would-be murderer. "I don't—understand," responds the murderer, and the arresting sergeant helpfully explains:

You mean about the "death?" Well, obviously the cartridges in the gun were blank. As for the rest—(HE *moves to the wall that contains the bloody matter*) Well, Phoebe is not only a good actress but is also experienced in the use of—(HE *flips panel around to wall so that the bloody matter has disappeared*) special effects. I rigged it myself earlier in the day . . . [18]

In traditional detective fiction, the detective is not above setting a trap for the murderer, especially as a part of the conventional reconstruction of the crime, but theatricalizing the scene to this extent, with blanks, false deaths, and, especially, a trick wall panel decorated with "splattered brains," surely represents an extreme example of police acceptance of the techniques of illusion and misdirection. For the viewer who finds credulity strained, however, the play still has a final turn to offer. In the final scene, all these events are revealed to have been "an act of the imagination," a playing out in the mind of a mystery author of a possible new plot.

As more and more graphic "details"—blanks, blood, brains, death agonies—are added to make the fake deaths more convincing, more and more elaborate preparation, on the part of the characters involved in the illusion, is necessary. While Milo Tindle, in *Sleuth*, obligingly fainted at the proper moment, later "victims," who must exhibit more elaborate death signs, have to be aware that they will be called upon to play the corpse and must prepare for this "role" with appropriate props and makeup. This necessity reinforces the triangular plotting that, as we have already noted, is so central to this genre. The false death is, of course, primarily set up to shock and mislead the audience, but it must also be justified, within the narrative world of the play, as a set up to mislead one of the characters. Clearly, to prepare his "trap," the "victim" must know when the "murder" is coming. Most obviously, this can occur when "victim" and "murderer" are in league against a third party, for whom the trick is staged, as in *Deathtrap*. Almost equally common, however, is the situation in *Stage Struck*, where the "victim" is in league with a confidant of the "murderer," who reveals the murderer's plans and allows the victim to put blanks in the gun, replace the poison with harmless pills, or otherwise defuse the danger, and then feign death in order to trick the would-be murderer.

In more recent comedy thrillers, the false death has itself become so predictable a part of the givens of the genre that it can itself serve as an element for subversion. During the late 1980s, Gerald Moon's *Corpse!, Sleight of Hand,* and *Accomplice* all, though in different ways, indicated this process at work. One might not agree with the opinion of the *Los Angeles Times* reviewer who observed, "If *The Mousetrap* is the thriller for the fifties; *Sleuth* for the sixties; *Deathtrap* for the seventies; *Corpse!* is surely the thriller for the eighties,"[19] but there is no question that each utilizes and parodies central strategies of its predecessors, in a series of increasingly elaborate traps for audience expectations. The false death, a single, central trick in *Sleuth* and *Deathtrap,* becomes a kind of running joke in *Corpse!* Evelyn, an out-of-work actor, hires Major Powell to murder his wealthy twin brother, Rupert, (both brothers are played by the same actor) so that Evelyn can assume his identity. When the major shoots Rupert, however, Evelyn fools him into thinking he has shot the wrong brother, apparently meaning to saddle the major with the crime. Rupert is not, however, dead; after the others leave, we see him recover. In the meantime Evelyn has gone to Rupert's flat, where he and Powell argue. Powell shoots the second brother, and is about to flee, when Rupert returns. Powell, who thought Evelyn was Rupert, now thinks Rupert is Evelyn, back from the dead. As Rupert attempts to flee this apparent madman, Powell shoots him again. The staggered major complains:

> There's another one! I've shot another one! This morning I hadn't heard of Evelyn and Rupert Farrant. Now I've killed them, both!

I've got to get out of this madhouse before I kill someone else! You never know—there might be triplets!

Now Evelyn appears from that favorite locale of resurrected victims, behind the sofa, to explain that "this time you've really killed him. No fake blood now!"[20] Evelyn then explains that the now empty gun contained first a dart tipped with curare, to stun Rupert but not kill him, then a blank, for his own encounter with Powell, and finally, a live bullet, which the major has just used on Rupert. This was all an elaborate plot to prepare evidence to suggest that Powell and Rupert had killed each other in a quarrel in Rupert's flat. Although the audience does not know until this explanation how the tricks have been managed, the series of false deaths functions primarily to provide humor at the confused major's expense. They have become an almost predictable element in the increasingly complex plots of such thrillers.

While *Corpse!* piles up false deaths with the kind of maniacal repetitiveness suggestive of traditional farce, *Sleight of Hand* offers false deaths in almost every scene, but in such profusion and variety that it might almost be called a set of variations on this theme. A brief opening scene shows a drunken magician, Paul, rehearsing the familiar swords-through-a-box trick, when blood begins to seep out of the box. "Oh, Jesus," he says. In the next scene he confesses to his girl friend, Sharon, that he has just killed his assistant, but when she throws open the box, it is empty. The story of the killing was only a trick to keep her at home. As she leaves in disgust, Paul threatens to kill himself, and indeed pretends to do so with a false sword. The audience, who almost certainly did not believe in the apparent death of the assistant in the opening scene, is thus confirmed in their assumption that the magician was simply playing another trick, as he continues to do throughout the play.

The major false death of *Sleight of Hand* double codes the by now well-established false death conventions of comedy thrillers, both following and parodying them, with a clear expectation of audience knowledge of and complicity in this process. After Sharon's departure, Paul practices several tricks, culminating in placing a rabbit in a press and apparently crushing it. As in the opening scene, blood seeps out, and as it does so, Paul's buzzer sounds and the speaker announces, "Police." A long scene, full of tricks and mental sparring between Paul and the mysterious "Dancer," who may or may not be a policeman, follows, ending with Dancer firing several shots into Paul's body and producing a satisfactory display of blood. Dancer then phones Sharon to say, "It's all over" and "I love you," and, with a final joke about the magic properties of the room, he leaves. Dancer's amusing final line, the revelation of the traditional triangle (the mysterious Dancer really Paul's romantic rival), and the first-act shooting, which an experienced audience will assume to be some kind of trick, sets up an act ending quite conventional for a play of this type, but *Sleight of Hand* surprises by showing that it knows that the audience knows the trick. Instead of dropping the curtain early to conceal the trick, as in *Sleuth,* the curtain is left up to reveal the trick as in *Deathtrap,* but with an even more conscious foregrounding of the ludic quality of the situation. When Dancer is gone, Paul reappears, unharmed and in evening dress, holding his equally unharmed rabbit, to whom he comments about "the illusion of life." His closing line is an invitation for everyone to go with him to the theatre.

The second act, which takes place at the theatre, begins with another echo of the opening scene; Sharon is seated in a spotlight, slitting her own throat, with blood running out, "Dancer," now revealed as Geoff, interrupts her rehearsal. Reluctantly, he tells her that their "joke" on Paul, turning his murder games back on him, went wrong, real bullets were in the gun, and Paul was really killed. She accuses him of attempting another trick on her. The audience knows that Paul is not dead, but this knowledge only produces new puzzles. Does Geoff really think

Paul is dead, and if so, how did Paul manage to reverse the plot? Or does Geoff know that Paul is alive, and if so, why is he lying to Sharon? Early comedy thrillers often changed the traditional mystery question from "who done it?" to "did the murder really happen?" Then, as audiences became accustomed to this destabilization, the original question came back, on a more theoretical level, "given that the murder is an illusion, who is controlling the narratization of it?"

The final scene of *Sleight of Hand* suggests, on a grimmer note, the frenzy of illusory death that characterizes Major Powell's endeavors in *Corpse!* Both Paul and Geoff appear in and disappear from a coffin. Blank pistols, stage swords, and trick blood are all utilized in a series of "deaths." At one point in the theatrical carnage, however, Paul, who during the play has been providing a running series of "lessons" on stage magic, pauses to interject a grimly serious, as well as strongly self-reflexive, note with his "lesson four," which he calls "the dark side of the soul":

> People don't realize that magicians wish to frighten. We deal daily with death . . . We delight in the murder as much as the resurrection. How close can I bring you to the edge without pushing you over? People pay me to prove to them that death is conquerable. But death is real and disappearance is pretend.[21]

At this moment, *Sleight of Hand* seems to reach outside its generic playfulness to touch upon a basic truth about the appeal of all such plays, and perhaps, of all theatre. For a moment, we seem very close to Herbert Blau's insight that it is the deferred knowledge of death that haunts and fuels all theatre, all performance. But if "death is real and disappearance is pretend," the theatre remains a process for the protection of life from this reality by its obsessive deferment, repetition, and reserve.[22] In the final scene of *Sleight of Hand,* Paul confesses that he really did kill Alice in the sword box in the opening scene. The most obviously false death of all was real. "I performed the ultimate trick," he boasts, "there was no trick." But the trick Paul plays upon Sharon, Geoff, and the unfortunate Alice is repeated on another level by the trick *Sleight of Hand* plays upon its audience, always the ultimate target of the murderer's illusions. Once the "false death" has entered the realm of generic expectations, as it has by now clearly done in the comedy thriller, it becomes as open to the play of a subversion as the "real death" of the traditional mystery dramas. "Reality" can be double coded onto "illusion" as easily as "illusion" onto "reality," when either can be anticipated as a codified interpretation. Although the entire middle section of *Sleight of Hand* is filled with trickery and surprise, such activity, because anticipated by its audience, proves, in fact, less surprising and less subversive than the beginning, where we see an apparent murder and a man who claims to be a detective who comes to investigate it, and the ending, where we find that our reception expectations have been mistaken because the text has, in fact, returned to the world of the traditional mystery—a murder really was committed, the man really was a detective, and at the end, the murderer is exposed and arrested.

This does not, of course, mean a return to the relatively straightforward world of the "fair-play" mystery, since the final effect of *Sleight of Hand* is to suggest that that world is a construct like any other—playing no trick is the "ultimate trick." As the calculating cardinal observes to the Pope in Anouilh's *Becket,* "Sincerity is a form of strategy just like any other, Holy Father. In certain very difficult negotiations . . . I have been known to use it myself."[23] In a world without ontological grounding, like the world of the postmodern, no transparently honest action is possible, and any "reality" may collapse into ludic misdirection and deferral. The conclusion of *Sleight of Hand* reminds thriller audiences, if they need reminding, that nothing, not even illusion, can be taken for granted.

6 STAGE STRUCK

"Think of it . . . a murder play in
which there *had* been a real murder: a whodunit in which one of the
actors on stage was a genuine
killer. Can you imagine the publicity it would get?"
—Sam in *The Butler Did It*

The detective fiction writer who decides to create a "real" murder plot has proven, as we have seen, a very popular trope in
the comedy thriller, and his role, as co-creator of the narrative
structure with the actual author, has proven a very effective
center for emphasizing the constructedness of the activity in
these plays. A somewhat different strategy is to call attention to
the other end of the dramatic process, not to the creation of the
script and the tension between reality and the dramatic text, but
to the enactment of that text in the theatre and the tension
between actor and character. This latter emphasis, where the
codes subverted are as likely to be theatrical as narratological
ones, has become increasingly popular in recent examples of
the genre.

The comedy thrillers of the 1970s, despite the theatricalization of their plots, with protagonists utilizing disguise, blanks in guns, stage blood, and rehearsed scenes for the mystification of other characters and of the audience, remained anchored in the fictive world of the traditional mystery. Three plays at the end of the decade, however, carried this theatricalization to such an extreme that they provided a kind of transition to the thrillers of the next decade, that literally moved from the country house or well-to-do apartment onto the stage. The peculiarly performative basis of the plot in Shaffer's *Murderer* has already been noted. The protagonist, Bartholomew, seeks to remove suspicion that he may be preparing to commit a real crime, by elaborately acting out famous historical murders in front of his windows where they can be observed by the neighbors (as well as by the audience). Bartholomew has, even more literally than Sidney Bruhl in *Deathtrap* the previous year, essentially converted his living room into a stage.

Robert, a former actor and the protagonist of *Stage Struck*, is even more obsessed with the theatricalization of his situation. While Bartholomew's conversation is full of references to famous, lurid crimes of the past, Robert's shows a similar preoccupation with theatricalizing the present. His confrontation with the presumed psychiatrist, Widdecombe, which occupies the entire center section of the play, is as consciously "staged" as is Bartholomew's false murder at the beginning of *Murderer*, but Robert also provides a running metacommentary on this. He begins the sequence by turning up the lights and converting the living room into a "stage": "I won't open the curtains if you don't mind—I don't like glimpses into the wings, if you see, it always looks so unreal out there—."[1] In the next scene, when Robert is menacing Widdecombe with a gun, he essentially becomes the director of the situation:

> ROBERT: . . . Sit down. (*Widdecombe goes to sit down*) No, not there. The sight-lines are terrible. (*Widdecombe moves to another chair*) Nor there—you'd be upstaging me. Now bring that chair over . . . (*Widdecombe follows Robert's instructions*)—that's right. And

put it there. I could make a good props man out of you, Widdecombe, if I didn't need you for a leading part.[2]

"Entrances" and "exits" are similarly theatricalized. "Darling,
you're on," Robert cries as he opens a trap in the ceiling and
lets fall a dummy that the horrified Widdecombe (and presumably the audience) temporarily assumes is Robert's murdered
wife, Anne. At the end of the scene, Robert drives Widdecombe
to shoot him, as Anne's car is heard approaching. Blood seeping
from his stomach, Robert observes: "Just—perfect—timing.
For—her—entrance. But—for—me—bring down—the curtain—
the tabs! *(He collapses slowly behind the sofa)*."[3] This is, as has
already been noted, another of the common false deaths of the
comedy thriller, complete with blanks in the gun Widdecombe
is driven to use and stage blood.

The "theatricalization" of the accompanying lines might be
taken as pointing to this convention, but, in fact, Robert continues to theatricalize, even when the death becomes real. The final
game in comedy thrillers often ends in real death, and *Stage
Struck* follows that rule. Robert continues to stage manage the
situation. He threatens to shoot Anne unless he is stabbed first
and, as he counts down the final ten seconds, urges Anne to
say her final words: "You've done Cleopatra, Hedda—just a few
lines to exit on. Don't worry about context." Anne is unable to
rise to the occasion, but Robert, stabbed and then shot when
Anne seizes the gun from him, manages very well, though with
a considerable assist from *Hamlet:*

> This is the first death speech I've ever been allowed to make,
> and look, I can taste it—real blood—and when they come tell
> them—of carnal bloody and unnatural acts—accidental judge-
> ments—casual slaughters, of deaths put on by cunning and
> forc'd cause, and in the upshot, purposes mistook fall'n on the
> inventor's head—and none of it—would have happened—if it
> hadn't been—stage-managed by—by—a—poet . . . *(He reaches
> out a hand to Anne—and dies)*[4]

Theatrical metaphors and vocabulary are extremely common in comedy thrillers, and sometimes, as in these two plays, are so pervasive as to keep the audience almost continuously aware of the actions as theatre. I have spoken, in an earlier chapter, of the narrative self-referentiality which many of these works share with the "narcissistic" postmodern novels and short stories analyzed by Hutcheon, but as performed theatre works, the comedy thrillers can and normally do take advantage of their opportunities for generic self-reflection on this level as well. Silvio Gaggi turned to modern experimental theatre for basic models of self-referentiality in his study *Modern/Postmodern,* suggesting that many postmodern works employ either a Brechtian or a Pirandellian approach to this activity. Most of the examples given so far have been self-referential in Gaggi's "Brechtian" sense; that is, "they employ a variety of devices designed to foreground style and otherwise remind the audience that what it is experiencing is artifice." The style "calls attention to itself and blatantly obtrudes itself between the viewer and the work's denotative content."[5] A few early examples of this genre and many of the more recent ones have, instead of or in addition to this "Brechtian" mode, also offered examples of "Pirandellian" self-reflexivity, making the fictive world, entirely or in part, a theatrical rehearsal or performance and playing with the tensions between the multiple levels of narration, or reality, thus introduced.

The move to another "level of reality" when a scene taken as "real" is exposed as "theatre" has a dramatic device with a history far earlier than its use by Pirandello. It is especially popular in periods of high artistic self-consciousness, like the baroque, and our own times. It is a device that is particularly well suited to the concerns of the postmodern, since the emphasis on the performance not only foregrounds the constructedness of the dramatic text but radically disrupts its move toward closure. Indeed, a number of recent theorists such as Josette Féral and Michael Kirby have looked to the interplay between the closed system of the dramatic text and the open flows of performance as the most effective site of postmodern paradoxical double-coding available to theatre.[6]

The theatre has long been a popular setting for stories of detective fiction. Each of the major woman mystery writers of the "golden age" of the genre—Margery Allingham, Agatha Christie, Ngaio Marsh, Dorothy Sayers, and Josephine Tey—were interested in the theatre and utilized it to some extent in their work. Over a third of Marsh's 32 detective novels have theatre settings, a world she knew intimately. The illusions, trickery, and disguise of the theatre event have naturally attracted authors in a genre built upon such concerns, and even the construction of the genre follows parallel lines, as Sue Feder suggests in the opening article to a special issue of the *Mystery Readers Journal* on "Theatrical Mysteries." "Pre-planning the murder is the equivalent of script-writing," Feder suggests. "Setting the alibi is like learning the role and speaking lines. The murder is the play."[7] The "theatre mystery" remains today one of the most popular sub-genres of detective fiction, and there are even several series featuring detective/actors: Simon Brett's Charles Paris, Linda Barnes's Michael Spraggue, and Anne Morice's Tessa Crichton, for example.

Somewhat surprisingly, mystery plays set in the theatre have been far less common, perhaps because traditional detective dramas, for all their participation in the world of illusion and misdirection, needed a fictive world with a solid base to support their variations on familiar themes. In the novel, the theatre, for all its trickery, is simply another specialized setting, not, in any basic way, different from the advertising agency, the college campus, the race track, or any other public location where a group of possible suspects can be assembled around a crime. In the theatre, however, the depiction of a theatre almost invariably raises Pirandellian questions about the status of the reality we are watching, questions that are highly appropriate to the self-conscious modern comedy thriller, but which would almost invariably be irrelevant and distracting in a more traditional piece. Among the dozens of mystery plays and thrillers that enjoyed at least some measure of commercial success on the stages of London and New York in the first two-thirds of this century, I have found only four actually set in theatres: Martin Fallon's *The Last Warning* (1915), Fulton Oursler and Lowell Brentano's *The Spider* (1926), Philip Barry and Elmer Rice's *Cock Robin* (1933), John Randall's *Reserve Two for Murder* (1939).

It is quite clear what made a theatre setting appealing to Fallon, whose *The Last Warning* in 1915 seems to have been the first detective drama with such a locale. Like Bayard Veiller and other early twentieth-century thriller writers, Fallon was at least as much influenced by the tradition of gothic melodrama as by that of investigative ratiocination, and although his detective hero, Arthur McHugh, solves the mysterious murder of a theatre manager, he does so by reopening the manager's theatre, now reported haunted, and staging a revival of *The Snare*, during a performance of which the manager met his death, with most of the original cast. Most of the action occurs in the theatre or on stage, but for Fallon, the stage is most useful as a domain of generated special (preferably horrific) effects—mysterious falling pictures and dropping sandbags, huge spiders crawling up the walls, disappearing bodies, cat eyes glowing in the dark, flame spurting from opened books, unlocatable cries and maniacal laughter, an actor found dead in a green spotlight. Although the audience is distributed a fake "program" for the presumed revival before the climactic second scene of the third act, this is really nothing more than an amusing gimmick. There are plenty of theatrical tricks and effects in *The Last Warning*, but the fictive world remains absolutely steady, and there is never any confusion or blurring between on and off-stage activity.

Fulton Oursler and Lowell Brentano's extremely popular *The Spider*, written a decade later, after the first professional productions of Pirandello had stimulated an interest in such experimentation, involved the audience in a much more radical way. Here major scenes were presented as if they were happening in the theatre, in the "real world" of the audience, though this experience was still very strongly qualified and theatrically framed. The audience who attended the first productions of this play at the 46th St. Theatre in New York, or later in theatres in Boston, Philadelphia, and elsewhere, came into an interior that was decorated to suggest a vaudeville rather than a legitimate theatre, a distinction that was still obvious in interior decor during the 1920s—national flags and bunting decorated the stage and boxes, ushers and ticket takers wore rakish hats with the legend "Tivoli Theatre" on them, and at either side of the stage were large potted plants and signboards to announce the individual "acts." Perhaps most striking, audience members were given a program, not headed "46th St. Theatre" but "Tivoli Vaudeville Theatre," which did not provide information about *The Spider* but listed a series of vaudeville acts—a newsreel, a skating act, a black-face routine, a magician. Presented in a traditional vaudeville fashion, these indeed are what the audience witnesses when the show begins.

Then, in the course of the magic act, comes the quintessential detective-drama stage direction: "ALL LIGHTS *stage and auditorium suddenly go out. The struggle and altercation continues in the dark. There is a* SHOT. BEVERLY *screams,*" and when the lights go on after a few moments of confusion "*On the steps, near to the feet of* CHATRAND *lies the twitching body of* CARRINGTON. *Blood.*"[8] The "manager of the theatre" appears onstage, two "doctors" come up out of the audience to treat the victim, "electricians" and "stage hands" run about, and a police officer, "Sergeant Schmidt" takes charge and cautions the audience to remain in their seats "until we find out what's happened here." All of this may suggest the experiments of Pirandello, but *The Spider* has nothing of the conflation of theatre and reality found in Pirandello's most self-reflexive works. Although the murder takes place on the liminal steps between stage and auditorium, presumably in the "real world" of the audience, that "real world" has already been carefully encoded as a fiction. The audience itself has been cast in a role, as the fictive audience of the imaginary Tivoli Theatre, and there is never the slightest suggestion that the murder might really have taken place in the actual theatre they are attending. The entire situation has been fictionalized. Interestingly, there is not even an ambiguity about levels of reality operating in the other direction, involving the fictive world of the stage, as would be the case if the "Tivoli Theatre" had been presenting a conventional play in which a murder occurred, and the question was raised as to whether that murder had happened in the play or in the "real world" of the Tivoli Theatre. Making the murder occur during a vaudeville turn removes this possible fictive ambiguity, just as bringing the audience into the fictive world removes the ambiguity of the performative situation. The vaudeville act, within which the murder occurs, does not create a separate fictive world, but exists on the same level of reality as the Tivoli Theatre, and thus as the audience.

At a period when Pirandello was still creating his more original works on such themes, *The Spider*'s device must have seemed striking and curious, and doubtless contributed significantly to the play's popularity, but in terms of destabilizing the genre or its fictive modes, it really was no more radical than *The Last Warning*. Indeed, though the lobby is filled for the first intermission with fake policemen who summon the spectators back to their seats under presumed orders from "The Inspector," the second act returns to a totally conventional mode of presentation. The stage no longer represents, iconically, the stage of the Tivoli Theatre, but, instead, a perfectly conventional illusionistic scene, a backstage dressing-room in that theatre, where the audience is, of course, forgotten. To complete the transition back to conventional theatre, the regular program for the production is distributed during the first intermission.

Cock Robin, except for a rather more distinct parodic tone, is closer to *The Last Warning* than to *The Spider*. The action all takes place on a stage, but during a rehearsal process, and the real audience has no fictive role to play. Still, at least two features of the play anticipate later thriller devices. The first is that the play opens with a theatrical scene, a duel in an eighteenth-century English grog-shop, which is played straightforwardly as a conventional drama until it is interrupted by a "director," who establishes another level of fictive reality. The second is the nature of the murder and of the murderer. The crime actually occurs during the grog-shop scene, which is repeated several times during the play, the last time with a leading character, Robinson, stabbed. Eventually, one of the actors, an amateur detective, solves the crime. The director himself, a former professional knife-thrower, committed the murder, as well as staging it. As Lane, who solves the mystery, explains:

> You've rehearsed this thing for weeks! You picked the play—cast yourself for this part—and carefully arranged the positions so that there'd be five people around Robinson, on whom suspicion would naturally fall.[9]

The bizarre solution clearly parodies the over-ingenious machinery of many whodunnits and, thus, rather suggests the opening of *Sleuth*, where Andrew sketches out a mystery solution similarly based on a most unlikely physical feat. The idea of the murder being "rehearsed" and "staged" (here, literally) is, of course, also an extremely common trope in the thrillers, adding to their interest in foregrounding the fictionality and constructedness of their actions. Finally, at the end of *Cock Robin*, the company comes to the highly unlikely decision that they will not reveal to the police what actually happened, because the victim deserved his fate. So, as is commonly the case in more modern thrillers, the police arrive as the curtain falls, with the audience aware that truth will not be discovered and the disruption of the crime resolved.

Reserve Two for Murder is less subversive of traditional mystery narrative than *Cock Robin*, though it is considerably more subversive of traditional theatrical conventions. Of these four plays, it is the one that makes the most serious attempt to dissolve the traditional clear division between stage and audience. As in *The Spider*, the audience is openly acknowledged as audience, but here a majority of the actors are seated in the auditorium and play audience members, and the action takes place in no imaginary "Tivoli Theatre," but presumably at the time and place of the actual performance (originally the Cherry Lane Theatre in New York). When the audience arrived, they were given a false program to a play with the title, *Reserve Two for Murder*, set five hundred years in the future and starring its presumed author, John Randall. This strange program was surely disturbing enough, but stranger activities followed. The curtain rose on a futuristic set with characters speaking a ponderous blank verse about relations between the sexes in the remote future. Not until several pages into the play do we enter familiar territory, and ironically, it is a situation traditionally conceived as totally disruptive that restores the confused audience to a familiar world:

> (*Suddenly every light in the theatre, stage and auditorium goes out, leaving the place in absolute blackness. A piercing* SCREAM. A SHOT *rings out from the Center aisle. Utter confusion*)[10]

When the lights go back on, the body of the "actor and author, John Randall" is discovered on stage, presumably shot by someone in the audience. From this point on, the mystery follows a fairly predictable path, under the able control of a detective sergeant and his Charlie Chan-like Chinese assistant. No further destabilizations of reality occur; indeed, once we leave the world of "John Randall's" futuristic drama for that of "reality," this continues until the end of the play. The audience remains involved throughout—shepherded into and out of the lobbies by police officers at intermissions, directly addressed by the police, and producing participants in the action from their midst—the play ends with the arrival of the homicide squad backstage to arrest the murderer. One assumes that the real world of the audience was restored with the curtain call, where the dead "John Randall" would reappear as the actor who played him, but the printed script does not say if this was done, and the final direction, that the lights come up on a drawn curtain with the police arriving behind it, suggests that this closure may not have occurred. Certainly, in more recent thrillers, the destabilizing of the fictive universe has often spread outward into the destabilizing of traditionally reliable framing elements, such as the theatrical program and the curtain call, and we can already see in such plays as *The Spider* and *Reserve Two for Murder* that the reliability of at least the first of these has already been undermined.

The theatre program is not generally thought of as a particularly significant part of the audience's experience in the theatre, but, in fact, in the case of a play with which the audience is unfamiliar, it normally provides a variety of important orienting suggestions, including the time and place of the action, the names (and often relationships) of the characters, and the overall structure of the action (act and scene divisions and placement of intermission). When the audience is called upon by the drama to fill the role of a fictive "audience," then a normal program presents something of a problem, as both of these productions recognize, by the utilization of a fictional program for the audience's fictive role. A similar device was recently seen in the theatre in the program for Michael Frayne's delightful farce, *Noises Off,* which also included the parallel program for the fictive play, *Nothing On,* which we were also watching as the "audience" at Weston-super-Mare.

In cases like these, the production of a dummy program, not at all designed to confuse the audience, but simply offered as a part of the game of make-believe, is a fairly straightforward matter, but the program and the expectations it generates have presented a more serious problem to subsequent mystery dramas and, not exclusively, to those that specifically experimented with the boundaries between levels of reality on the stage. One of the traditional conventions of the theatre (indeed so generally followed that until it is disregarded one does not think of it as a convention), is that the program provides accurate and truthful information about what will be offered on stage. This "authoritative" text, external to but still inescapably tied to the stage world, can, even for the writer of a conventional detective drama, provide a hindrance unlike anything experienced by the writer of regular detective fiction. If conventional program usage is followed, an author of detective drama cannot, for example, keep an audience in suspense about whether a particular character will make an appearance or not, since the program will reveal this. Nor can a character appear in a major assumed role without being exposed by the program. As questions of identity and reality become more central in modern thrillers, the existence of a grounding location of authority, even in so tangential an aspect of production as the program, has become a problem and eventually has resulted in the program becoming subverted by the instability of the fictive world.

An early example of potential tension arose in Agatha Christie's *Witness for the Prosecution* (1954), where the major surprise in the play (and the film) comes from the audience's not being aware that the wife and the "other woman," whose testimony provides a surprise defense for the hero, are in fact the same person, played by the same actress. In a conventional theatre program, this trick would be revealed, but the highly ingenious conclusion to the play not only gives an unexpected turn to the narrative but also solves this information problem. In the final moments, a real "other woman," who is a different person, played of course by a different actress, does appear. By the time the audience realizes that this is the "other woman" mentioned in the program, and not the false witness played by the wife, that more fundamental trick has already achieved its effect.

Shaffer's *Sleuth* bases one of its major surprises on a similar trick, the audience's assumption that "Inspector Doppler" is a new character, not the perhaps dead Milo Tindle in disguise. The structure of Shaffer's play does not allow the covering of this dilemma with an ambiguous phrase like "The Other Woman," so the problem is solved in a more radical manner, by a direct lie in the program. An imaginary actor, Philip Farrar, is listed as playing the role, and, since the conventions of the American theatre program require the inclusion of a brief biography for each actor, this fictive personage must also be provided with a fictive biography. Nor is this the end of the matter. After Milo reveals his trick to Andrew, he initiates another contest, warning Andrew that real police will be coming, at his invitation, to question Andrew about a "real" murder that Milo claims to have committed and planted incriminating evidence of in Andrew's home. As Andrew searches frantically for this evidence, Milo announces the arrival of the police, and goes offstage to let them in. We hear Milo speaking to the two policemen in the hall, then returning to the room:

> MILO:*(Enters)* Come in, gentlemen. May I introduce Mr. Andrew Wyke. Andrew, may I introduce Detective Sergeant Tarrant and Constable Higgs.
> ANDREW: Come in, gentlemen, come in. *(A pause. No one enters)*
> MILO: Or perhaps I should say Inspector Plodder and Constable Fishface. Thank you, Sergeant. We shouldn't be needing you now.
> TARRANT'S VOICE: That's alright, sir. Better to be safe than sorry, that's what I say. Good night, sir.
> MILO: *(Own voice)* Good night, Sergeant. Good night, Constable.[11]

Once again Milo has tricked Andrew and, it is hoped, the audience, but again the trick will be exposed if the program lists no actors to play the imaginary Tarrant and Higgs. Therefore false names and biographies also appear for these characters, creating what is surely an unprecedented situation in the history of the theatre, a program in which more than half of the listed cast are imaginary, with equally imaginary biographies.

This degree of program subversion is extreme, but after *Sleuth*, audiences for comedy thrillers could no longer expect the program to serve its traditional role as a secure, if modest, grounding for the fictive world they were about to enter. Terence Feely's *Murder in Mind* (1982) contains three major characters who claim to be the husband, sister, and cousin of the heroine, but whom she insists are impostors. Since the ambiguity of this situation fuels much of the play, the program seeks to emphasize it by listing the contested names in quotation marks. A note in the printed text explains "It is suggested that the names of the characters should appear thus in programmes to preserve the suspense of the play, although these names are printed normally in the text of the play."[12] A misdirective strategy opposite to that of *Sleuth* was employed in the program to Eric Elice and Roger Rees's *Double Double* (1986). As *Sleuth* covered two of its major plot turns by adding to the program names of authors and characters who in fact never appeared, *Double Double* protected the surprise of its final scene by *not* listing in the program the name of a character who *did* appear. Here too, a note in the acting edition emphasizes the importance of this strategy:

> It is our intention that no mention should be made in the programme that the character of Richard James appears on stage. It is also our intention, though again it should never appear in the programme, that the same actor portrays the roles of Duncan McFee and Richard James.[13]

There is an interesting tension between the pressures of commercial concerns and audience expectations that are invested in a contemporary program and the restraints that the assumptions of this program place upon the character instability in many modern comedy thrillers. *Solitary Confinement* provides a particularly striking recent example of this. All Broadway theatres now use a mass-produced program, the *Playbill*, appearing each month and using the same advertising and general articles for every play, but with the covers and certain pages given over to a specific production. Page 23 of this mass-produced program is the essential bill, listing theatre, producers, director, author, title, cast, and designers. On either page 24 or 26 (if there are cast pictures on 24) there is a list of roles and the actors who play them, a note on the time and place of the action, and the number and length of intermissions. The biographies, or "Who's Who in the Cast," begin on page 29. It is unlikely that even the most alert reader of the *Solitary Confinement* program would notice, before the production, that page 23 lists only one actor, the star, Stacy Keach, even though six other actors are listed in the cast and provided with biographies in the "Who's Who." Generally, no New York agent representing any of these actors would allow this to occur, but in this case, the situation can be explained by a conflict between program practice and thriller subversion. The fact is that, as in *Sleuth* and *Double Double,* actors appear in the program who do not appear on stage and, indeed, one actor apears on stage who is not listed as an actor in the program.

The disjuncture that this sort of experimentation has introduced between the program and its presumed referent, the physical performance, has affected not only the security of the audience reading of the program text, but other readings beyond the performance itself. The professional organization, Actors' Equity, which used to require a copy of the program for its records of professional participation in specific productions, now requires further depositions or sends representatives to productions to be sure that the Actors' Equity records show who is actually performing.

The conversion of the program into a fictionalized "program" and of the audience into a fictionalized "audience" involves the same foregrounding of the performative situation that stresses the "theatricalism" of the action being witnessed. *Murderer* and *Stage Struck* perform this foregrounding metaphorically and linguistically, but rather surprisingly, none of the comedy thrillers before the 1980s literally reveal themselves as theatre. Interestingly, the two plays that do carry out this more extreme project, Stoppard's *The Real Inspector Hound* and David Fulk's *The Potman Spoke Sooth*, are both offered not as direct contributions to the mystery genre but as parodies of it.

The distinction between a "serious" postmodern work and a parody is often a rather vague one. Indeed, as I have already noted, Linda Hutcheon in her study of postmodernism considers parody in certain ways the perfect postmodern form, in its simultaneous installation and subversion of accepted codes and procedures.[14] In terms of playfulness with conventions and generic self-consciousness, there is really not a great difference between these two "parodies" and more recent works that have styled themselves as main-line "comedy thrillers" such as *The Butler Did It, Sleight of Hand,* or *Accomplice.* If a distinction can be made, it would surely have to be on the somewhat difficult grounds of what the play seems to be seeking in terms of audience response. Despite the strongly comedic tone of both comedy thrillers and parodies, the former is still much concerned, on some level, with generating suspense and shock, while the latter is devoted only to laughter and ridicule. The characters and situations in comedy thrillers may be artificial, the murders often false, but they encourage an attitude of at least qualified seriousness from the viewer. There is little of the attitude of spoof generated, for example, by the sobriquet of the unknown criminal in *The Potman,* the "Peanut Murderer," or by the insistence of Mrs. Drudge, the domestic help in *The Real Inspector Hound,* in referring to her surroundings arbitrarily as the "charming though somewhat isolated Muldoon Manor."

Each of these plays, however, has strong similarities to later, more metatheatrical comedy thrillers. Despite its complex play with illusion and reality, *Hound*'s final trick is to take its games seriously, ending with "real" shootings and the exposure of a "real" plot involving the "real" characters in the play, the dramatic critics. Despite the ubiquity of false deaths in comedy thrillers, these plays almost invariably end with a real death, which, as in this case, takes on an ironic appropriateness in view of the entire action of the play. What makes Stoppard's play unique among metatheatrical detective plays is his emphasis on the critics, so that the process of public reception and the interplay of personal and professional concerns in this reception provides an important dimension of the drama. Later metatheatrical pieces, such as *The Butler Did It* or *Accomplice,* remain "within" the production apparatus, dealing with the interplay of actors and directors with the fictive world they are creating.

In this respect, *The Potman,* though a much less ambitious one-act spoof, more directly anticipates the dynamics and concerns of later comedy thrillers. Its greater emphasis upon false deaths and similar theatrical tricks is also doubtless due to the fact that *The Real Inspector Hound's* inspiration came only from the traditional Agatha Christie type of stage mysteries (especially *The Mousetrap,* which by 1968 had already been running sixteen years in London), while *The Potman,* in the mid-1970s, was directed to a public that had already witnessed the first modern comedy thrillers, in particular the ground-breaking *Sleuth* of Anthony Shaffer.

Although *Hound* plays throughout with the tension between the "real" world of the critics and the "fictive" world they are reviewing, *Potman's* strategy is more a *mise en abyme,* setting up a series of "real" worlds, only to subvert each in turn. The play begins in the "typical" sitting-room of a "typical" English country home with the characters discussing the "typical" maniac killer loose in the vicinity, in short, much the opening of *The Mousetrap,* or for that matter, the internal play in *The Real Inspector Hound.* A police inspector arrives, the lights go out, and the woman of the house is murdered, but then the play begins to deteriorate. None of the four characters seem to be what they appear, and each accuses another of being the murderer. At last, they interchange shots and all fall dead.

Immediately thereafter, they all arise and reveal themselves as a retired British couple, a butler, and a neighbor who play "murder games" (rather as Bartholomew does in *Murderer*) to amuse themselves. Shortly after, they seem to be drifting into another "game," with various characters waving guns, confessing to being the murderer, and revealing that the tea has been poisoned, but in the midst of this, the confused "wife" refuses to continue, saying that she cannot understand the play they are in. "Let's face it," she says, "we're actors, that's an audience, it's a theatre, it's a bore . . ."[15] At this point, approximately halfway through the play, we seem to have reached the level of "reality" that supports the play-within-a-play we were watching at the beginning. As the actors argue about how to get back into the action, a "policeman" arrives to arrest them, explaining to the audience that the actors they have seen are not actors, but escapees from a local mental institution who have tied up the real actors backstage.

As the policeman attempts to remove the "actors," a "director" with clipboard and script comes out of the audience to stop the production. He reveals that the policeman is, in fact, part of the script, but begins criticizing his performance. This discussion is again interrupted, now by the "playwright" who claims the director is an impostor. The policeman asks if this is part of the play, inspiring this dialogue:

> DIRECTOR: . . . this is not part of the play. This is really happening!
> PLAYWRIGHT: Wait a minute . . . are you sure that was your line?
> DIRECTOR: Of course it's my line. Why else would I say it?[16]

"Audience members" begin to complain and are accused of "jumping their cue." Finally, the playwright appeals to authority. Nothing can happen in the play unless he writes it. The others reluctantly agree to this, when a new voice is heard—a woman in the light booth who the playwright insists he did not write in—who demands that the playwright leave the stage. At this point, no one on stage can be sure they exist, since all grounding—the text, the author, the director, even the production process—has been challenged. The playwright shouts an appeal to "Anybody" to stop this process. In response comes thunder, a blackout, and a deep echoing voice:"WHO ARE THESE THAT DARKEN COUNSEL BY WORDS WITHOUT KNOWLEDGE?" "Thank God," responds the playwright, and rightly so, for the words are, of course, God's, the opening of his mighty response to Job's suffering, a response that in fact does not explain, but places the workings of the universe beyond human comprehension.

The *mise en abyme* has apparently been stopped, in the most traditional manner, by the voice of God, the ultimate grounding and source of authority. God dutifully carries out his obligation, "naming," and thus entitling, the playwright, the directors, the actors, even the woman in the light booth, so that an order of authority is re-established in a theatrical universe that had come perilously close to dissolving in postmodern jouissance. The Voice even obligingly provides the solution to the murder, thus re-establishing the moral order of the fictive universe: "THE BUTLER HATH DONE IT." A bit of concern might be felt by the actor/characters about the predictability of this response, but that is a small price to pay for the certainty of a ground in the universe. As the wife remarks, echoing a concern common to many contemporary conservative critics and readers: "All I can say is, thank God there's a final authority on these things." Unhappily, even the deity is overtaken by theatrical artifice. As the actors are departing, the Voice cries: "HOLD! THOU SHALT RUN IT FROM THE TOP, AND PLAY UNTIL THE MURDER-ERRR IIISSSSS RRREEEUHHHH. . . . The Voice grinds to a halt, the lights return to normal, and the woman in the booth announces that "the tape broke."[17] The disillusioned actors, deprived of this last hope of authentication, despair of narrative closure and fall back upon theatrical closure, taking a curtain call and departing.

One might question whether, ultimately, *The Potman* is really best classified as a parody of mystery dramas, since the specific

genre, and indeed all generic questions, disappears midway
through the play to be replaced (except for the final accusation
of the Butler) by a more general parody of the theatrical process
itself and by a comic playing with the impossibility of discovering in the modern world, and perhaps especially in the
modern theatre, any reliable ground of authority. Several of the
more recent comedy thrillers have explored this same theme,
some with almost the same degree of epistemological destabilization and parodic subversion as *The Potman,* but they have continued to maintain, even on different levels of "reality," the
concerns of this specific genre. This provides another reason for
considering them, despite clear parodic elements, primarily as
comedy thrillers, in the tradition of *Sleuth* and *Deathtrap,* rather
than as theatrical parodies in the tradition of *The Real Inspector
Hound* and *The Potman Spoke Sooth.*

The high degree of generic self-consciousness in Anthony
Shaffer's *Whodunnit* has already been noted, especially in respect
to the characters in that play. Although the play features actors,
disguised as traditional mystery "types," and a detective,
dressed as John Dickson Carr's Dr. Fell, who participate in the
staging and then the restaging of a murder, the context is not
presented as, precisely, a theatre, but rather something more in
the manner of a modern "mystery weekend," where actors assume roles and commit a crime to be solved by other participants. Thus, most of *Whodunnit* does not involve the sort of
playing with the phenomenological situation of being in the
theatre that we have been considering in other plays. Only the
Voice of the Murderer that, like *The Potman'*s Voice, speaks over
the loudspeaker out of the darkness to provide a kind of guide
and authority, seems to acknowledge the fact that all of this is
taking place in a theatre before an audience. At the end of the
play, the police leave the stage, confessing themselves baffled,
and the gloating voice of the murderer has apparently the last
word. However, matters are resolved on another level, when the
inspector returns during the curtain calls and arrests the actor

who had been playing the butler, explaining how only he had a serious motive to kill the victim. When the murderer confesses and is being taken away, the inspector reveals that his inability to solve the crime within the play proper was due to his "theory of the non-culpability of servants in dramatic literature," but that he was right because, despite the cliché, this is surely the first time that the butler truly did do it.[18] This makes a satisfactory curtain line, but hardly a stable conclusion, since the inspector does not arrest the butler, but the actor who played the butler, whose motive was as an actor in "real life," not as a blackmailed character in the "play." Indeed, it was only by moving, not only outside the world of the "play" but also outside the play containing that play, into the liminal world of the curtain call, that the inspector was able to reject his dependence upon generic expectations and discover the real criminal.

The move to an acknowledgment of the theatre that occurs only in the curtain call of *Whodunnit* erupts in the opening scene of Walter and Peter Marks's *The Butler Did It* and, thus, becomes much more integrated into the dramatic action. Scarcely has the action of *The Butler Did It* begun when the first murder takes place, but scarcely has that occurred, when we see the "dead body" of "Mrs. Butler," hidden in a window seat by the others, crawling offstage behind the setting. Another character stops the action and comes from the auditorium onto the stage. We find that this is the presumed director and author, Tony, who reveals that all we have just seen is a rehearsal for his new whodunnit. In the ensuing sequence, Tony sets up with the actress who plays the victim, Mrs. Butler, a false death, known to the audience but unknown to the actors, to encourage in them an experience of "authentic" feelings. The other actors, and then the audience, are subsequently led to believe that Tony's "fiction" has turned into "reality," and a detective appears to investigate the actress' "death." Only after the actress makes a surprise, and very theatrical reappearance, arising once again from the fatal window seat, now bathed in a special spotlight and with a piercing scream, does Tony confess that he also planned this extra turn and that the "Detective" is another actor, who will in fact play the detective in the play.

After these games, *The Butler Did It*, though still focussed upon the preparation of a play, settles into a more conventional pattern, until near the conclusion. Several of the characters are given strong motivations to wish harm to Natalie, including Tony himself, who actually tries twice, unsuccessfully, to poison her. What gives this sequence its strongly metatheatrical flavor is not that it takes place on a stage and involves actors and a director, but that its dynamics have been laid out in some detail as theatrical constructs in the second scene. In a passage somewhat reminiscent of Dr. Fell's disquisition upon locked-room mysteries in *The Three Coffins*, Tony holds forth on distinctions between whodunnits and thrillers, especially on how each generates suspense:

> Let's say a character enters . . . *(He begins to act it out)* picks up a cup of Sanka . . . drinks and . . . *(Clutching at his throat, collapses)* . . . dies. That's a whodunit. The suspense comes from the audience wondering *who* put the poison in the Sanka. The murder has to be real. It's the central driving-force in the play, because all that really matters in a whodunit is . . . who-*dunit*. It's so important, in fact, that if the audience knew who the murderer was, there'd be absolutely no point in them seeing the play.
> NATALIE: What happens in a thriller?
> TONY: In a thriller you've got a different kind of suspense. *(A beat)* Let's say that I take the cup of Sanka . . . *(Acting it out)* . . . reach surreptitiously into my pocket . . . and put poison into the cup—which the audience sees. Then I offer it to *you* . . . *(Extending the cup to NATALIE who takes it)* Now the audience is feeling . . . "My God, Natalie . . . don't drink the Sanka!" That's a thriller. The audience knows you are in mortal danger.[19]

Although the play, *The Butler Did It*, that Tony has written and is rehearsing is presumably a whodunnit, *The Butler Did It* that we are watching, in which Tony is a character, is in fact a thriller, and so, according to his own formula, Tony's attempt to poison Natalie is set up so that the audience is fully aware of what is going on, and, indeed, not only Natalie but two other actors almost drink from it before the rattled Tony gives up and throws it away. The climax of the play and the rehearsals is approaching. Tony, speaking Mumford's climactic speech, reveals the murder method, a book with pages coated with poison that the victim picked up, licking her fingers while reading, but the rehearsal ends before Tony reveals the name of the murderer. Soon after, Tony, left alone, again starts to put poison in Natalie's cup, but he is surprised by Claudia. He spills the poison on his clothing and has to brush it hastily away. Claudia wishes to go over a scene with him, and as Tony licks his fingers searching for the place in the script, he realizes with horror that he has poisoned himself. Yet, ever the professional, he calls the actors together and, semi-reclining on a couch, gives a melodramatic death-bed speech: "It's time for the final curtain, for me to tie all the loose ends neatly together," he observes, but although he informs the actors that one of them has murdered him by poisoning his coffee, he refuses to name the guilty party. His final gesture is to convert the "reality" of his death back into the fiction of a whodunnit, but in the guise of "real life." "In a classic whodunit the murderer is always caught," he concludes, "but this is not a play, people. This is real life."

> The police will never be able to solve this case. You'll all be suspects for the run of the play. And with the publicity we'll get, it's going to be a long, long run. *(Struggling to his feet)* Call Lester. Tell him I've finally come up with a handle. We'll be on every front page. "Whodunit Director Slain. The Butler Did It!" (TONY *collapses on the couch and dies*)[20]

Snatching victory from defeat, Tony presumably gains success for his whodunnit, which will name the murderer and tie together the loose ends to establish the ordered universe of that genre by the support of what is actually, by his own definitions, a thriller, in which the poisoned Sanka, for all its foregrounding, is a red herring, in which the dead return to life, and in which the murderer is known to the audience but never discovered by the police. Tony, of course, never realizes that he is in a thriller; he stresses, even in his final line, that this is not a play, but "real life." The line makes no real claim to audience belief. We know perfectly well that Tony's situation is not "real life," and yet his claim has some merit. Every fictive world tells us something about the real world as well, and just as the classic detective story told us about a real world of justice and order, the thriller tells us about a real world where such matters are much more problematic, where what we take for substance may be theatre, and where it is by no means certain that the forces of order and reason will be able to "solve the case."

This undermining of "reality," so common in the comedy thriller, is not carried out extensively in *The Butler Did It*, despite its theatrical setting. After the tricks of the opening scenes, attention shifts more to developing suspense in the manner Tony describes, and the audience's interest is maintained in that manner, not by any further confusion as to what is truth and what illusion. When the police investigate, they will probably not be able to discover "the truth," nor will any of the survivors in the play, but we in the audience know the truth, and this gives to the play's events a kind of stability and ground which is lacking in a more freewheeling playing with the theatrical process like *The Potman Spoke Sooth*. Rupert Holmes's *Accomplice*, a more recent and more elaborate experiment, brings such instability into the main line of comedy thriller writing, offering the audience no secure ground from the opening curtain (or indeed before) through the final curtain calls. Although *Accomplice* is essentially another example of the "theatrical" comedy thriller, its elaboration of the generic strategies is so complex that it deserves separate consideration.

7 THE AUDIENCE AS/ FOR ACCOMPLICE

"We have to keep startling the audience in a desperate attempt to keep one step ahead."

—Hal in *Accomplice*

Rupert Holmes's *Accomplice* is one of the most recent and surely the most extreme of the comedy thrillers, in the variety and complexity of its playing with the established codes, both of the mystery play and of the comedy thriller itself. A survey of its strategies may therefore provide a kind of summary of the current state of this increasingly self-reflexive genre. As the characters in *Accomplice* remark, in an embedded discussion of the genre somewhat over half-way through the play, audiences do not come to comedy thrillers planning to play the old and fairly straightforward game of trying to guess the murderer but to play the more complicated game of trying to stay a step ahead of the tricks and misdirections the author presents to them. Returning again to Barthes's distinction of texts, the pleasure is not in movement toward a conclusion but in the playfulness of each individual sequence.

Instead of watching for "clues" to identify the murderer or the crime, a thriller audience comes to the theatre watching for tricks to be played on them as to the nature of the "reality" being presented to them on the stage and, at times, in the auditorium as well. Nothing can be regarded as reliable, least of all the most secure conventions, codifications, and assumptions of a traditional theatre or mystery play experience, since it is precisely the most transparent assumptions, through their subversion, that provide the richest material for audience surprise.

Nor is the subversion restricted to the discourses of the performance itself. Since every element of the theatrical event contributes to the reception process, and the disruption of conventionality of that process is a goal of the genre, then any element in the event under the control of the performing apparatus may be subverted. A particularly striking example of this is the program, which as early as *Sleuth* we saw being used to provide false information to mislead audience reception. A distinction must be made between the handing out of obviously false programs, as in *The Spider* and *Noises Off*, and the handing out of what seem to be authentic programs that contain false information, as in *Sleuth*. In the former case, when the audience receives a program for another play in another theatre, they realize that they are playing the role of a fictive audience and can frame their response accordingly. When they are given a program that seems to represent the correct play and theatre, they can be expected generally to accept its truthfulness.

Of course, games of this sort, like the false deaths so common in comedy thrillers, must keep changing in order to maintain any hope of surprising an audience, which today will almost certainly include a significant number of people who have some experience with the tricks of this genre. Probably some such members of the audience suspected misdirection at work in the unconventional cast listing of *Accomplice*. The *Accomplice* program was a conventional *Playbill*, the middle section of which is devoted to the specific production. Four actors were listed in order of appearance, but with no accompanying character assignments. Although the first scene was announced as "The moorland cottage of Derek and Janet Taylor," the program, in defiance of normal custom, did not reveal who was playing either of these parts. The alert audience member might, from this, have been able to guess that at least some of the evening's trickery would result from a subversion of the traditionally stable bond between actor and character, and such a guess would have been absolutely correct, though surely no audience member could have guessed at the extent of this activity.

Other, subtler departures from normal program custom, also marking sites of subversion, surely passed quite unnoticed. Following the cast listing came the usual statement headed STAND-BYS: "Standbys never substitute for listed players unless a specific announcement for the appearance is made at the time of the performance." In a normal *Playbill* this announcement is followed by a listing of the standbys with the roles they are backing. The *Accomplice* program provided no listing, but instead included biographies for five standbys, like those traditionally provided for the regular actors. Another unusual element was a note at the bottom of the Cast page, "The cast of ACCOMPLICE dedicates their performance in this production to Crystal Matthews." Such dedications are unusual, though not unheard of. Crystal Matthews would be an unknown name, but the careful program reader would find, in the last sentence of the biography of the author, Rupert Holmes, an identification: "Holmes dedicates *Accomplice* to his late sister, Crystal Matthews." Probably none of these departures from traditional program practice attracted particular notice, but each, like the false names in the *Sleuth* program, actually marked an encroachment of fictionalization into the real world of the theatre event.

Even those audience members who suspected some misdirection in the rather unconventional style of the program were doubtless fooled when *Accomplice* "colonized" or "fictionalized" a different element of the normal event reality in which the actual performance is embedded. The curtain was held a few minutes past the announced time for the play to begin (not an

uncommon phenomenon in the Broadway theatre). Then came
an announcement over the theatre P.A. system: "Ladies and
gentlemen, we apologize for having held the curtain a few extra
minutes and we thank you for your patience. At this performance of *Accomplice*, the part normally played by Mr. Michael
McKean will be portrayed by Mr. Paul del Gatto."[1]

Such announcements are not at all uncommon in the professional theatre, and on the occasion this writer saw the play, this
was received, as is usually the case, with some muttering and
disappointed groans from the audience. The disappointment
was surely that of not seeing the usual actor, but a substitute,
however, since though McKean has a solid reputation as a film
and television actor, *Accomplice* is by no means a star vehicle,
where the loss of the leading actor might be cause for audience
members to consider requesting a refund. Surely no one suspected that the play had already begun and that this announcement, like the pseudo-biographies in the *Sleuth* program, was
not a communication in our world, but a part of the dramatic
web of illusion. Paul del Gatto, a stand-by whose "biography"
appeared in the program, did not, in fact, exist, and the actor
we were about to see was, in fact, Michael McKean, a reality
never admitted by the production until the final curtain call.

Having thus set up several hidden interpretive traps, *Accomplice* apparently began in a highly conventional manner. Its
elaborate and comfortably monied setting was recognizably in
the tradition of such plays, and the opening pantomime of the
Man of the House arriving home from work and mixing a drink
suggested nothing out of the ordinary until the man abruptly
stopped the pantomime and, turning to the audience, observed,
"That's *exactly* how all those *plays* begin, isn't it? 'Dorping Mill,
the renovated moorland residence of DEREK and JANET TAY-
LOR. . . .'" He then went on to repeat precisely the opening
stage directions he had just enacted.[2] This conversion of the
verbally suppressed side text of stage directions into a part of
the spoken text of the performance constituted, of course, a

radical breaking of traditional performance codifiction and, like the opening of *Deathtrap,* offered, through the device of self-reflexivity, a foregrounding of the theatrical process itself and its play of illusion. The opening of *Accomplice* works in a somewhat different and phenomenologically more radical manner, however. In *Deathtrap,* what we find is a character within a play apparently reading a copy of that play; a hall of mirrors that, despite its epistemological instability, remains contained within the world of the play. *Accomplice* brings the instability across the footlights into the relationship between actor and audience, challenging the stability of the dramatic illusion itself. The actor, unlike Andrew in *Deathtrap,* seems to have replaced Eco's first performative statement, "I am acting," with another, "I have just been acting," to call our attention to the arbitrariness, artificiality, and already-writtenness of what we have just witnessed, from a position of "reality" which he seems now to be claiming to share with us.

As we shall see, this challenge to the codification of the theatrical illusion itself is highly germane to the overall development of *Accomplice,* but this opening jolt, like almost everything that happens in this play, is not what it seems to be. Although the actor has intellectually "stepped back" to comment upon the theatricalized quality of the actions he has just performed, he has not, as the audience is led to assume, done this by stepping outside the fictive world of the play to speak to us as an actor. He is, in fact, like Andrew in *Deathtrap,* still in the fictive world, speaking not to us but to another character, still offstage. A stage direction explains how this quick "coding" of a presumed direct address must be retrospectively "recoded" into a more conventional indirect one: *"this rather loud soliloquy, which we thought was addressed to us as some sort of Brechtian prologue, was instead directed towards* JANET, *who was offstage."*[3] Janet now appears and addresses the man as Derek. Those who recall the program will now be able to identify these two as Derek and Janet Taylor, the owners of the moorland cottage which is the setting displayed, and since the cast was listed "in order of appearance," one can assume that Paul del Gatto (the standby) is playing Derek, since Michael McKean was the first name listed, and that Natalia Nogulich is playing Janet, his wife. This assumption, however, is based upon the normal operation of naming codes, and like most assumptions based on normal code operations in *Accomplice*, is later revealed as mistaken.

An essentially realistic scene ensues, full of verbal sparring and ending in Janet telling Derek she has poisoned his drink. He drops to the floor, apparently dying, as Janet disposes of the incriminating glass. Experienced viewers of comedy thrillers may suspect that this "murder" may not turn out to be real, and they will be correct, but the particular circumstances of this false death resist further codification. Janet seems to hear a noise that we do not hear, then rushes to the door to welcome in two people invisible to us, "Jon" and "Melinda," telling them that Derek has had some sort of attack. The stage directions note that *"this is not played as hallucination, but rather as if these additional people were invisible to our eyes."*[4] Janet and the invisible "Melinda" start to put a blanket over the "body" of Derek, who suddenly reaches up, seizes Janet by the neck, and pulls her down violently. The gesture and dynamic of the scene suggest the return from the "dead" of Clifford in *Deathtrap*, seeking revenge on his "murderer," reinforced in *Accomplice* by a struggle beneath the blanket. But then there is silence and laughter, and the blanket falls away to reveal "murderer" and "victim" in a passionate embrace.

Their subsequent dialogue reveals that what we have just witnessed was, in fact, not Derek's homecoming, but Janet and her lover, Jon, rehearsing the murder of Derek, her husband, who will arrive later in the afternoon. This elaborate and carefully prepared surprise, a kind of comedy thriller equivalent to Becque's famous opening to *La Parisienne*, indicates how the modern comedy thriller has moved from a double-coded fulfillment and subversion of the conventions of traditional detective fiction, to a similar simultaneous fulfillment and subversion of the expectations of the comedy thriller itself. Most of the basic generic elements of this sort of play are utilized in this opening surprise—the false death, the mistaken identity, the elaborate plot, the rehearsal of a crime, and for that matter, the basic situation of a death plot against one member of a sexual triangle. The audience has even been warned, by the opening line, of the sort of generically self-reflexive games that are going to be played in *Accomplice,* but this knowledge only increases the effectiveness of the surprise.

The close relationship between the actual events of the action and a theatricalization of them continues to inform the characters' lines. Janet remarks to Jon that she got the idea of using nicotine as a poison from a theatrical thriller, remarking: "Really, you should go to the theatre more often, Jon. There's life in it yet."[5] After Jon leaves, and Janet is tidying the room, she discovers a hidden tape recorder and, replaying it, hears the incriminating conversation she has just had with Jon. The last words we hear on the recording are those where she tells Jon about her idea of using nicotine: "I saw it in a play. A thriller. . . ." A fast blackout and the traditional thriller punctuation, a clap of thunder, end the scene.

The second scene of the first act combines two familiar strategies from other thrillers. Now that we have seen the mechanics of the plot against Derek, we can use this foreknowledge to follow the actual plot as it unfolds, and, as invariably happens in such a situation, suspense is increased as various things go wrong and Janet is forced to improvise. Particular attention is given to the attempted poisoning, as Derek again and again evades Janet's attempts to force a drink upon him. As the director warned us in *The Butler Did It,* this particular device is a standard thriller technique, but Janet's discovery of the hidden tape introduces a calculated ambiguity into the interpretation of this otherwise familiar situation. Since we know Derek is suspicious enough of Janet to tape her conversations, it is possible that his continual failures to accept the drink are not simply by chance, but calculated. At the end of the sequence, Derek reveals that he in fact has been aware of the poisoning attempt, but until this point, the audience should remain balanced between two alternative interpretations of what is happening, a consideration so important that the script contains an "author's note" urging that the audience remain uncertain about Derek's knowledge of the plot until this point.[6]

The state of Derek's knowledge is revealed when Janet accuses him of "playing a little game" with her, and when he pretends not to understand, she elaborates:

> JANET: I'm talking about my attempt to murder you.
> DEREK: What attempt to murder me?
> JANET: I mean the poisoned drink.
> DEREK: Oh *that* attempt.
> JANET: With your corresponding gambit of "let's not drink the drink."
> DEREK: Yes, I thought I might be laying that on a bit thick myself.
> JANET: Especially since you've had such a good chance to study the script in advance.

At this point she switches on the hidden tape recorder, and we hear her voice and Jon's from the first scene, plotting Derek's murder.[7]

Thus the "poisoning" sequence, theatricalized in the audience's mind by the first scene "rehearsal" they have already witnessed, is revealed to be theatricalized by the characters as well, both of whom are playing "roles" based on that "script." Like the characters in *Sleuth* or *Murder by the Book*, they seem even more interested in playing games of illusion and reality than in pursuing the kind of through line of action that is traditionally offered in dramatic narrative. Why, we may wonder, did Janet continue with the plot after she had discovered the tape and knew Derek would be warned? In terms of effect, the answer is, of course, that this introduces an effective instability in the audience's attempt to codify and interpret what is happening.

Within the fictive world, however, a by-now familiar strategy is being followed. The classic dramatic struggle between different actants has become, in large part, a struggle of wits, an intellectual game in which the moves are based on misdirection, illusion, and manipulation of reality; the stakes concern who will control what is accepted as "reality," and the "game" being played between characters on stage stands in for a parallel game being played between author and audience. Given the self-consciousness of the genre, it is hardly surprising that this situation is specifically articulated at one point in *Accomplice:* one character observes that the audience is already speculating about the "real" motives of another character, suggesting, "You know how the audience loves to be one step ahead in a thriller." "You're kidding me?" another exclaims, "It's like a chess game between you and . . . the audience."[8]

Scarcely has the "poisoning" sequence been revealed as a game, than another apparently begins. Janet threatens Derek with what seems to be a gun wrapped in a towel. Both he and the audience are naturally suspicious of this new "threat," and indeed Janet very quickly "fictionalizes" the new situation, saying that she and Jon, knowing Derek's suspicions, staged the murder conversation as a trick on him. The "gun," she reveals, is only an electric hair dryer. Just as Derek (and the audience) are tempted to look back on everything they have seen this far, the murder plot included, as part of an elaborate (if somewhat questionable) joke, Janet suddenly tosses the hairdryer into Derek's footbath and plugs it in, giving him a fatal electrical shock. Just at the moment when fictionalization seemed established, a "real" murder is committed. Scarcely has Derek died, in a grimly realistic electrocution, than Jon and Melinda arrive, and the previously rehearsed scene with them is rapidly played out. The death plot, first presented as real, then recorded as a trick, abruptly is revealed as real after all. One final turn, however, brings the act to a totally unexpected conclusion. When Jon leaves in a fruitless (and previously rehearsed) attempt to summon medical aid, Janet and Melinda, left alone, do not simply place a blanket over Derek's body, as Janet showed in the "rehearsal," but move into a passionate embrace and kiss. When they finally break apart, Janet gives the shocking curtain line to the first act, "Half done!"

The stunning effect of this moment rivals the surprise near the end of the first act in *Deathtrap*, when the audience understands that their interpretation of everything that has happened up to that point has been built on assumptions suitable to conventional narrative but incorrect in this particular case. The trick again is based on two characters staging a false situation to delude a third (and the audience), and in both plays a hitherto unsuspected homosexual relationship not only aids the surprise, but also disturbs the audience's comfortable assumptions about the play's congruence to traditional personal relationships. Once again, *Accomplice* both fulfills and subverts the conventions of earlier thrillers like *Sleuth* and *Deathtrap*, just as these both fulfilled and subverted the conventional expectations of earlier detective drama. Audiences, accustomed to the strategies of comedy thrillers, expect false deaths, an expectation both fulfilled and undermined by the first act of *Accomplice*. When the long-planned death finally arrives, its manner of happenng is a surprise, and the audience is fooled, not by a false assumption about the "reality" of this death, which they were expecting, but by an assumption that seemed unproblematic, about the organization of the murder plot itself and against whom it is directed.

Despite the threatened destabilization of theatrical codes in the opening sequence, the first-act trickery of *Accomplice* all remains within a single fictive world of Derek and Janet's cottage. The second act, however, systematically leads us into an ever greater subversion of theatrical, as well as narrative, codes, primarily by turning the conscious theatricalism of the genre back upon itself in a series of increasingly radical undercuttings. This act is set, according to the program, a week later, and seems at first to continue the concerns of act one, but during the first scene, between Jon and Janet, a bizarre event occurs. The presumably dead Derek enters through the kitchen door, unnoticed by the others, and paying them little attention. He looks about for a moment, then picks up a flashlight left by the fireplace in the previous act, and exits. The puzzlement of the audience is extreme. The reappearance of a character coded as dead is, as we have seen, not at all uncommon in this genre as a part of an internal plot. According to this system, the "murder" of Derek would have been in fact staged by Derek and someone else, as part of a plot, yet to be revealed, against one of the other characters. Even this explanation, however, does not at all accord with Derek's casual entrance. Quite the contrary, generic expectations would call for a spectacular and highly theatrical reappearance, causing at least shock and consternation and, at most, fatal heart attacks in the other characters, a convention so widespread that it was specifically parodied in *The Butler Did It*.

The audience is really offered no interpretive strategy for understanding Derek's appearance until several minutes later, when an explanation is provided by a movement entirely outside of generic expectations. In a developing sexual scene between Janet and Melinda, Melinda partially undresses and then refuses to continue. In response, Janet calls out a new name, Hal, and this signals a shattering of the play's traditionally constructed world of illusion. The fireplace and flat behind it pivot in a half-circle, revealing the back of the set, with the word ACCOMPLICE stenciled on it. The actor who played Derek appears on stage through this opening, and the ensuing dialogue reveals that what we have been watching all evening is, in fact, a New Haven rehearsal of a new thriller, *Accomplice,* hoping for a Broadway run and that "Derek" is, in reality, Hal, the author and director of the production. Such a subversion is not original with *Accomplice,* even among comedy thrillers; much the same "turn" takes place in the first scene of *The Butler Did It.* The shift in levels of reality is more surprising here, however, because such a long and elaborate action has already taken place, and since (unlike *The Butler Did It*) the "staged" action of *Accomplice* has been presented in essentially a realistic and convincing manner.

In a sense, the play has come back to repeat its opening trick on a deeper level. Then, the audience, watching a rehearsal for a murder, took it for reality. After that reality (a stage reality to be sure) was established, it in turn was revealed to be a rehearsal. What we have seen is a series of three fictive worlds, embedded within each other, and in each, we have accepted the fictive reality, only to have that reading strategy subverted by the exposure of another ontological level. A variety of technical devices, such as a change in accents, mark this shift of fictive worlds. When "Jon," at the beginning of the play, is playing "Derek," he does so in "an immensely affable and charming 'British-old-school-tie' accent."[9] When he becomes "Jon" he speaks in a rougher, more working-class British accent, described in the stage directions (interestingly enough in theatrical terms) as a "Room at the Top northern or Michael Caine cockney."[10] As Brian, the actor in New Haven, he speaks, as do the others, with an American accent.

We are now situated in a new fictive world in which metacommentary about the play *Accomplice* is possible, even though it is carried on by a director and actors who are themselves still fictional constructs. One of the most familiar modern examples of a drama largely set in this terrain is Tom Stoppard's *The Real Inspector Hound,* which engagingly intertwines the fictive world of Muldoon Manor with the fictive metaworld of the reviewers, Birdboot and Moon. In terms of the actual generation of the fictive world, however, the stakes are higher in *Accomplice* because Hal and the others have the power to create that world, or whatever version of it we are permitted to see, while Birdboot and Moon, as reviewers, have only the power of reacting to a world created by others, not only in their original role as reviewers, but even later, when they are drawn into the fictive universe itself as characters.

On their newly revealed level as director and actors, Hal and the others are able to undertake a metatheatrical discussion of the progress of the play so far and the difficulty of keeping the audience off balance. They speculate on what the audience at intermission will anticipate, with Brian, for example, suggesting that a lot of them will feel that Derek, despite the onstage electrocution, is still alive, since "it's logical to assume that, what with only four actors in the cast, no death is real until at least midway Act II."[11] There is also discussion of the past careers of these actors, including a certain amount of intertextual playfulness. Brian, for example, notes that he has previously appeared in a variety of real and imaginary thrillers—"*Sleuth, Dial M for Murder, Write Me a Murder, Stage Blood, Stage Fright, Mousetrap, Deathtrap, Death Mouse. . . .*"[12]

After some discussion of a variety of problems with the script and with Harley, the actress playing Melinda, the "rehearsal" resumes, taking up the final scene, which is set in a different location, a suite in Claridge's Hotel. One of the interesting features of this section is that the audience is reminded that the stage setting itself has no more secure reality in this shifting universe than the characters. The detailed interior of "Dorping Mill" has already been revealed to us in a totally unexpected guise, not the iconic sign of a real British interior, but the iconic sign of a stage setting in New Haven representing a British interior that is no more "real" than it is. To further foreground the arbitrariness of this representation, Hal conjures up an imaginary Claridge's setting utilizing elements of the cottage interior. "We'll just rehearse the Claridge's Hotel scene here in the middle of our Dartmoor cottage," he announces. The actors (and the audience) are called upon to utilize the "imaginary puissance" summoned up by Shakespeare to turn the visible setting into something quite different. This transformability of theatrical signs is deeply embedded in theatrical practice, as such pioneer semioticians as Honzl and Bogatyrev observed,[13] but this is, conventionally, a practice of non-realistic theatre, totally at variance with the high degree of scenic iconicity in the realistic tradition, of which the thriller is a part. We are now asked to see the cottage couch as a glamorous art deco daybed, other furnishings are now supposed to represent imaginary chromium lamps and bookshelves, one door, though still physically present, "ceases to exist," the kitchen door becomes the door to the bedroom, and so on.

The closing scene of Act Two in the "Hotel" setting is now rehearsed. The lines and motivations are highly improbable and unbelievable, as is "Melinda's" concluding stabbing of "Janet." Under Hal's direction, however, the "realism" suddenly improves, as a stage direction indicates:

> MELINDA *raises a knife above* JANET, JANET *screams and the knife plunges into her heart.* JANET *bolts upright in horror and blood gushes across her blouse. It's all so skillfully done that even the audience isn't sure whether this is for real.*[14]

As soon as this realistically coded moment is completed, the action on stage diverges. "Melinda" and "Jon" give the scene's final lines in a "hyper-theatrical" manner with maniacal laughter. At Hal's cry of "Curtain! End of Act Two," they immediately stop and begin exchanging notes on the scene just played. As they are playing an action going from "realism" (the stabbing) to theatricalism (the lines following the stabbing) to realism (on a higher level, critiquing the scene just played), the actress Erika has continued to play the realism of stabbing straight through, so that it now converges with the realism of the post-rehearsal situation. She does not join in the comments of the others, but, unnoticed by them, slides lifelessly from the couch *"realistic blood seeping into her shirt."* The audience is thus offered two contradictory post-stabbing codings of the stabbing. Hal and the others, by the metacommentary on it, have framed it as fictive, while Erika, continuing to exhibit the signs of a real stabbing, offers a simultaneous and contradictory coding of reality. Finally Harley notices Erika's situation and touches her fearfully. Erika suddenly sits up, laughing at her "joke." "Now *that's* acting," observes Hal approvingly. What has made this little sequence particularly destablizing, however, is not simply that Erika's feigned death was effective, but that it provided one of two simultaneous stage "realities," each of which deconstructed the other.

With these alternative realities again consistent, the "real life" of the actors continues. The empty-headed Harley and shrewish Erika depart for lunch, and Brian and Hal begin tidying the stage. As they fold up the blanket, repeating the action of the two women at the end of the first act, Brian impulsively kisses Hal, jolting the audience with a replay of the homosexual turn of the first-act curtain, on this new level of reality. We now find that the New Haven rehearsal has itself turned into the plot of a comedy thriller. Hal and Brian have planned, in a distorted reflection of the plot in Hal's play, to murder Hal's wife, Erika, in a rehearsal "accident." What we have just seen happen in "jest," they plan to carry out in "earnest." The weapon is to be the trick knife wielded by Harley, jammed so that its blade does not retract. Hal hopes to benefit from this scheme on both a personal and professional level. Like many a comedy thriller protagonist, he has organized an elaborate and theatrical plot to rid himself of an unwanted spouse, and like the protagonists in those thrillers with a particularly theatrical bent, he also sees the commercial possibilities in this crime. The publicity from a death during rehearsal would be enormous, what he calls "the best career move Erika ever made."

When the women return, this plot moves forward, the audience now anticipating a "real" murder in the "theatrical" framework, but once again expectations are thwarted. The unpredictable Harley, apparently by accident, does not stab Erika with the rigged knife, but the unsuspecting Brian, now bound and gagged in a chair as part of the New Haven script.

He exhibits all the signs of a death-agony, but the others seem strangely undisturbed, even Hal, who presumably knows that the knife is dangerous. Harley, far from sympathizing with Brian's apparent agony, characterizes it as "really bad acting." The explanation of these apparently inappropriate reactions is brought about by another shift in the level of reality. Harley now refers to "Erika" by another name, "Natalia," which is in fact her real name (the part was played in New York by Natalia Nogulich). Natalia then speaks to a member of the audience, who comes up to join them on stage. He is shortly after introduced as Rupert Holmes, the actual author of *Accomplice*.

Holmes and the actors, all now using their real names, explain to Paul del Gatto, still tied in a chair (and indirectly to the audience), that they have now left "the propped-up world of the theatrical thriller," where "blood is paint and knives retract and no death is final until the final curtain" and entered the real world of the Richard Rodgers Theatre on 46th St. in New York.[15] This entire production, we are now informed, has been organized as a trap to gain revenge on del Gatto for his contribution to the suicide of Holmes's sister, the Crystal Matthews to whom the production was dedicated. Presumably, up until this particular evening, the play had gone on to its regular conclusion (whatever that may have been), but this entire alternate universe is now explained as an elaborate trap for the understudy, set to spring, as it has this evening, when the leading man was unable to perform.

We have now reached the point in a traditional mystery, near the end of the final act, when the detective, in the presence of the suspects, goes back through the action to put together the clues he has observed that will point to a solution. In a sequence parodying this activity, the author, actors, and director (the potential murderers) point out to their victim, del Gatto (and to their other victim, the audience) clues scattered through the play pointing to the sister, her suicide, and this hidden plot. These clues however, found no detective to read them, and so the plot has apparently succeeded. Once again, now on the level of "reality," a murder is threatened, staged, but, presumably, really fatal, to which the real audience will be witnesses. Pamela Brull (who had played Harley) reassures the audience that no *real* harm is meant: "Three more minutes and you'll step out the door onto 46th Street, stroll east to Broadway for a drink at the Marriott Marquis or west to have a bite at JR's, and you'll smile at all this silliness." Jason agrees—"We're performing a play at the Richard Rodgers Theatre. Everything we're saying is in the script, Rupert showed the changes to the stage manager, the lighting crew has been advised of the changes . . . read from it, will you, Natalia?"[16] Natalia obliges, beginning her "reading" with the speech Jason just delivered, and going on with light, sound, and scenery cues.

Thus the normally invisible machinery of theatrical production is again foregrounded, but with more disturbing implications than in the New Haven sequence. Of course the audience was aware that the presumably spontaneous rehearsal discussions in New Haven were in fact scripted, since they still remained within a fictive domain. The audience knew it was not seeing a rehearsal in New Haven but a performance in New York, performed not by Hal and his actors, but by the real-life Jason Alexander and his colleagues. Now, with the world of the performance moved to the real Richard Rodgers Theatre on 46th Street, with actors and author representing themselves, this reminder of a controlling script places the audience back in a domain of calculated ambiguity—not about whether what they are watching is reality or not (though that is the apparent concern of the dialogue)—but about whether they are to apply a reception strategy that accepts it as reality or one that recognizes it openly as a theatrical performance. In terms of theatrical models, the world of Stoppard's *The Real Inspector Hound* has been left for the more radically unstable world of Pirandello, in such plays as *Tonight We Improvise*. The revelation, for example, that even Jason's self-reflexive line is written in the script ("Everything

we're saying is in the script . . . read from it, will you, Natalia?")
does not resolve the ambiguity, but in fact emphasizes it.

The reintroduction of the controlling script is perhaps particularly unsettling on this level of iconic identity, where actors,
theatre, and production are representing themselves. Yet on this
level, too the script is repeating a pattern of subversion already
established on other levels. Jon's repetition of his own stage directions in the opening scene was preparation for the subsequent revelation that this apparently realistic sequence was, in
fact, a theatrical fiction within the world of a Dartmoor cottage.
The repetition of the stage directions early in the second act
provided evidence that the apparently realistic Dartmoor cottage
was itself a theatrical fiction within a play rehearsal in New
Haven. The emphasis on pre-existing lines and stage directions
here functions, as in *Tonight We Improvise*, to prevent the audience from being entirely comfortable *either* with an interpretation of planned "theatrical" events or spontaneous "real" ones.

The climax of this sequence in *Accomplice*, like the climax of
the closing sequence of *Tonight We Improvise*, is, fittingly, an ambiguous death, occurring in the questionable area between the
fictive world (here of the New Haven rehearsal) and the "real"
world of the present production in New York. The angry del
Gatto, released from his bonds, rushes across the stage to attack
Rupert Holmes, the author. On the way, he falls into an electri-
fied trap and is apparently killed. Rupert approaches the body
to remind him that this trap had been "pointed out to your
character in Act Two Scene One as being the one element in
this set that's all real."[17] Del Gatto's apparent "error" was the
error of us all, in assuming the normal workings of fiction and,
thus, not suspecting that "real" information was being provided
to his "fictive" character. Thus his death has apparently been
the result of a misunderstanding of performative discourse. The
other actors hasten to assure the audience that this was a regret-
table accident and not in fact in the script, hardly a reassuring
line since we have just seen the demonstration that all these

effects, in fact, have been in the script. In the final line, the actor Jason Alexander nevertheless thanks the audience for accepting the role of a "lifelong accomplice," who, presumably, has witnessed a suspicious death on stage but will not report it to the authorities.

The curtain call, as Bert States has noted, serves the important function of returning the actors to our world of reality, a "means of dramatizing the all-but-forgotten truth that art has only used nature, as a parasite uses a host."[18] The curtain call in *Accomplice* returns, at last, to this traditional function, though some untangling of the multi-level complexities is still necessary. The first curtain call remains within the final level of reality of the play, very close to our own, with the "dead" del Gatto remaining motionless in the trap. For the second call, this actor joins the others in a more traditional bow. Then one of the actresses raises her hands for silence and explains, "for the record," that there is no such person as Paul del Gatto and that the actor so introduced was not an understudy, but the actor originally assigned the role, Michael McKean. The gentleman from the audience is also introduced as the actual author of the play, Rupert Holmes, though not possessed of any wronged sister. Thus, the last fictive frame of the production has been established and revealed, entirely outside the normal operating world of the production, as a fictive frame that began with the false biographies and other false information in the program and the apparently real, but actually fictive, announcement of the replacement of McKean by his standby, and ended *after* the first curtain call.

A striking feature of *Accomplice,* as of much postmodernist art, is that its code-breaking is not restricted to internal codes, but extends to external codes—in theatre the framing and performative codes—that have traditionally been seen as devices for identifying the ontological and phenomenological status of a work in a world of other events and objects and for providing clues and strategies for experiencing it. During May of 1990, moviegoers in some 250 theatres in the New York area saw an unusual filmed advertisement for *Accomplice* beginning with the notice, "Not coming to this theatre; not coming to any motion picture theatre." This ingenious trailer suggests how far code subversion has gone in *Accomplice*, since the fundamental surprise is possible, phenomenologically, only in the live theatre, where each production is unique and the last-minute appearance of a standby is possible. The film version of *Sleuth* has been accused, by some, of lacking the power of the stage version, but a film version of *Accomplice* is literally impossible, since it depends at its heart on the subversion of uniquely theatrical codes.

The progress of the play and its major turns can, in retrospect, be seen to have involved the establishment and the subsequent destruction of a whole series of levels of fictional reality, each embedded in the next and each employing its own set of validating codes. The real Michael McKean appeared from opening curtain to curtain call as his standby, Paul del Gatto, the victim of a fictive on-stage "accident" arranged by his fellow actors and his playwright. Del Gatto in turn appeared in the New Haven plot as Brian, conspiring with Hal to set up a fictive rehearsal "accident" for Erika. Brian, in turn, appeared in the play being rehearsed as Jon, who schemes with Melinda for the murder of both Janet and Derek. Finally, in plotting the death of Derek, Jon assumes that role for a rehearsal of the murder. Well might the play open with a discussion of the theatricality of its beginning, for the actor then speaking is in fact Michael McKean playing Paul del Gatto playing Brian playing Jon playing Derek. The role-playing, disguise conventions, and manipulation of reality that have come to be associated with the modern comedy thriller have been extended in *Accomplice* to a Genet-like house of mirrors.

In the reception of any dramatic performance, the audience enters into a kind of ontological game with the event, bringing certain generic expectations and being prepared to learn the rules of new codes unique to this performance. Clearly, a certain balance between predictability and surprise is essential. If the audience becomes too proficient in the anticipation of theatrical developments, they become bored and lose interest. If the events cannot be codified by the audience at all, there is a danger of frustration and irritation. The comedy thriller, as a genre, plays at the very edge of this second extreme, since the overriding generic expectation is not, as in the more traditional detective drama, suspense, but rather, surprise. There will quite likely be unexpected developments in the traditional "whodunnit," but the major source of mystification concerns the conclusion, and audiences are traditionally urged not to reveal the ending. Although the ending is certainly a surprise in *Accomplice*, the effect of the play obviously comes from the series of surprises scattered throughout, and the play's major "secret,"—its shifting levels of reality—begins to be revealed early in the second act. Thus, in a final line (delivered after the second curtain call), actor Michael McKean urges the audience to keep secret not only the ending, but the entire plot:

> please remember that you are sworn to keeping our twisted plot a secret. Promise now to seal your lips, or you shall forever cease to be our most trusted ACCOMPLICE.[19]

This request was amusingly reinforced on the posters for the production, which included the comment, "The show everyone's (not) talking about."

This final request provides one final occasion to call attention to certain principles of the theatre experience, always operative, but foregrounded in a highly self-conscious work like *Accomplice*. The title of the play itself, like the characters, shifts apparent referents as the fictive reality of its surroundings changes. By the time we reach the New Haven rehearsal, author/director Hal quite consciously uses the arbitrariness of this signifier to hint to each of his three fellow actors that they have the "title role." When "Paul del Gatto" is "killed," the audience itself is cast in the role of accomplice, through their presumed future silence in not revealing this crime, and though it is not very likely that this appeal will be taken as operative in the outside world, it is shortly followed, on the final level of performance, by another appeal for the audience to become accomplices by maintaining silence in the outside world, now about the plot of the play.

Most of the audience (unlike the author of this book) will probably be faithful accomplices on this level, but the term contains further implications beyond its ingenious and multiple use in the play itself. From the very beginning of the evening, the audience, in a very real sense, has served as accomplices in the complex game of mystification that is central to the effectiveness of this genre. A comedy thriller, as Jon and Brian observe in the New Haven interlude, is like a chess game between actors and audience, with elaborate rules known to each, but within which rules the actors attempt always to remain a step ahead. The audience must know the rules of this complex game (including not only the expectations of regular theatrical performance but the highly formalized and often calculatedly misleading strategies of the detective drama and its subgenre, the comedy thriller) and must utilize these rules to construct continually a series of hypothetical explanations for the strange events on stage, paradoxically deriving their great pleasure from discovering that their hypothetical constructions are again and again subverted by the evolving action. In the comedy thriller, the real victim is the audience, set up again and again to be mistaken in its interpretation of the fictive reality. The drama itself, of course, provides the calculated ambiguities, the misdirections, the deliberately false impressions, but the audience for such a drama must accept and enjoy being drawn to false conclusions, misled, and ambushed. This undoing of competencies, this deconstruction of the reception process, is by no means disturbing or troubling to the audience but is a source of pleasure, derived from the playfulness of the game itself. As Tani observes of the metafictional anti-detective novel, the "detective game is rarefied and intellectualized to such an extent that it becomes the sophisticated ritualization of the timeless game between writer and reader."[20] For the deathtraps to be sprung, the audience members themselves must help set them, through the play of intertextual and generic expectations. In this last, and ultimately most profound, sense the audience is indeed the production's "most trusted accomplice."

8 PIGS AND ANGELS: THE POSTMODERN PRIVATE EYE

> "I'm just a prisoner of genre, baby."
> —Taxi in *In a Pig's Valise*

The classical whodunnit, as developed into the British cozy, has provided the model for all of the works so far discussed, and variations of this form make up by far the most popular sort of detection drama on the modern stage. As the examples already discussed have indicated, the closed and highly regulated structure of this form, its predictable generic conventions, its easy adaptability to the conventional salon/living room of the modern realistic drama, and, perhaps especially, the battle of wits between its protagonist, antagonist, and the reader/spectator, have all contributed to making the cozy the type most subjected to postmodernist experimentation. Indeed Michael Holquist, in arguing that the detective story is to postmodernism what the structural and philosophical presuppositions of myth and depth psychology were to modernism, specifically excludes the hardboiled American detective story as an "impure exception" to the main line of the classic detective story, whose close relationship to postmodernist experimentation he is tracing.[1]

Certainly, it is true that private eye novels, while as highly codified as classic whodunnits, have, for a variety of reasons, not been similarly utilized by modern experimental writers, nor have they, even in more straightforward form, inspired much interest in the theatre. Almost every season brings new comedy thrillers, as well as more conventional mystery dramas, to the stages of London and New York, while private eye dramas remain rare. Nevertheless, the New York stage has very recently seen several examples of such drama, both on and off Broadway. Significantly, none of these provided a faithful imitation of the rich tradition of private eye dramas, films, and novels of the past, but like the comedy thrillers, all utilized, at least to some extent, the predictable conventions of the genre for parody, subversion and generic self-reflexivity. Perhaps it is not coincidental that the least successful of these was also the least committed to such experimentation. In any case, the fact that audiences had come to accept, and perhaps even to expect, this sort of metatheatrical game-playing in traditional detective drama, was surely part of the encouragement to these authors to extend the closely related private eye in similar postmodern directions.

One of the major technical problems in bringing this genre to the stage is its normal multiplicity of scenes, a convention, as mentioned before, that makes private eye pieces more naturally suited to film (where indeed the film noir is a major subgenre) and cozies to the stage. Contemporary audiences are not accustomed to frequent scene changes, necessarily utilizing fragmentary or suggestive scenery, in modern spoken theatre. This type of staging is, however, very common in the modern musical comedy, and that is doubtless one of the reasons why all of the recent private eye productions on the New York stage have been in the otherwise rather surprising form of musicals. Successful private eye musicals appeared both off and on Broadway in 1989: *In a Pig's Valise* by Eric Overmyer with music by August Darnell, and *City of Angels* by Larry Gelbart with music by Cy Coleman and lyrics by David Zippel. Late in 1991 came the often postponed and ultimately not well received *Nick and Nora* by Arthur Laurents with music by Charles Strouse and lyrics by Richard

Maltby, Jr. The following year came *Gunmetal Blues* by Scott Wentworth with music and lyrics by Craig Bohmler and Marion Adler.

Instead of the realistic interior, traditional for the thriller, these productions all utilized more abstract and artificial settings, all evoking Hollywood or Hollywood films of the 1930s and 1940s. The immediate inspiration for *Nick and Nora* was specifically the six stylish *Thin Man* movies of that era based in turn on the characters of Dashiell Hammett's final book, and the settings were stylized representations of various, mostly elegant, settings in the Hollywood film world. *In a Pig's Valise, City of Angels*, and *Gunmetal Blues* were more specifically evocative of the film noir of the 1940s, the locus classicus for visual images of private eye narratives. *In a Pig's Valise* began with an evocation of the typical milieu of such films—the cold, obscure, and grim streets of the inner city—represented, as is common in music comedy, by a collection of scenic synecdoches:

> Lots of fog.
> A streetlight. A couple of neon signs. Pale pink 'n
> blue neon fluid script.
> Heartbreak Hotel. Bar.
> Music: Opening Titles, a smoky instrumental, sax solo,
> something slow sultry sweet sexy sad and blue.
> The music starts and swells. The fog drifts and swirls.
> The sign flashes: Ba Ba Ba Ba Ba Ba Ba.
> A car approaches. Headlights. Fades away. Brakes screech
> on rain-slick streets.
> A match is struck. With panache.
> A man steps out of the fog. You know what he looks like:
> slouch hat, thread-bare suit, five o'clock shadow, no tie.
> Under his suit jacket he's wearing a pajama top instead of a shirt.[2]

These opening stage directions make it clear that the effect sought is not merely generic predictability, but a highly self-conscious generic predictability. Indeed, David Lehman's description of the film noir setting is so close to the opening of *In a Pig's Valise* that one might assume (incorrectly) that he had the play in mind in writing it:

> In forties *films noirs* the hard-boiled novel found its perfect pictorial complement: a chiaroscuro world of dark angles and elongated shadows, rained-on streets on which a solitary walker pauses to light his cigarette and a flickering neon sign punctuates the night.[3]

The audience of *In a Pig's Valise* was, however, clearly meant to realize that all of these clichéd signifiers of the film noir were being ostended in an obvious and unmistakable fashion and to read them not as signs for a sleazy, fog-enshrouded, city setting, but as signs for the sort of detective fiction associated with such a setting. The striking of the match "with panache" and the assured "You know what he looks like," underline the self-conscious, displayed quality of these recycled images.

A stage direction after the opening song by Taxi, the private eye, stresses again the expectation that the audience will read the visual image not as mimetic of life but of the fictionalized world of popular culture:

> *He lights up. The smoke from the cigarette curls up in the blue streetlights, and his cool pose is the essence of a classic forties album cover.*

Lest the audience miss this visual reference, Taxi's next line underscores it:

> It was two-fifty-two in the fretful A.M. I'd been ensconced in the back of my Chevy Bel-Air, dreaming I was a fresh-pressed Sinatra seventy-eight, with classic forties water-color cover art. Pastels.[4]

Gunmetal Blues opens on a set suggesting a seedy bar, the Red Eye Lounge, but this familiar type of setting is layered with ambiguity. The only person on stage at the opening is the pianist, Buddy Toupee, who, like Taxi, begins with a direct address to the audience, but in a more ambiguous role, which he maintains throughout. The theatre audience is frankly accepted by Buddy as "his" audience, and for them he plays a kind of narrator/master of ceremonies (later he announces the intermission, in the course of which he offers, to the audience, disks of his tunes and 8 × 10 glossy photos of himself for sale). Within the theatrical narrative, however, he plays all the roles not taken by the detective and the blond—a police lieutenant, a doorman, a cabbie, a telephone operator, a gangster—always at the piano where he can provide appropriate accompaniment.

Buddy's opening song specifically identifies the audience as voyeurs, linking the Red Eye not only to late hours and to "private eyes," but to voyeurism, a subterranean theme of the film noir itself (most notably brought to the surface in Michael Powell's disturbing cult classic, *Peeping Tom*). Thus film, theatre, detective fiction, and the reception process are linked together at once in a highly self-conscious way. These motifs established, Buddy introduces the setting and characters. As he speaks, a striking young woman with long blond hair enters, carrying a suitcase and wearing a trenchcoat. As she sits and lights up a cigarette, Sam, the private eye, enters with a trenchcoat slung over his shoulder, wearing the usual hat and loose tie. Says Buddy: "He's the eye in the nostalgia. He's Sam." Sam then begins the action in the typical speech of the long-suffering private eye: "It was one of those grey days in the city. I should have known it was going to be trouble."[5]

The opening of *City of Angels* foregrounded its derivation from the private eye film most directly of all:

> During the overture, the curtain rises to reveal a full-color movie poster, center:

> COMING SOON
> CITY OF ANGELS
> A BUDDY FIDLER PRODUCTION

> As the overture ends, three gunshots are heard. The movie poster fades to black and white. We hear an ambulance siren, hospital corridor sounds. The movie poster dissolves and flies.

The first scene in a hospital corridor is then revealed, indicated only by an overhead light and a hospital gurney with a body on it, wheeled in by an orderly. The voice of private eye Stone is heard over the scene:

> No sense kicking about death. No point arguing with the ump. For my money, checking out in your sleep gets the nod, the big nod, every time.

The elliptical, slangy, metaphorical, "hard-boiled" style utilized in each of these opening speeches is, of course, modeled directly on the verbal techniques of the "classic" private eye novel, as developed by Dashiell Hammett and Raymond Chandler. Like most of the other characteristics of the genre, this style of speech itself becomes a topic of discussion from time to time, as in the following interchange about one of the most typical features of the genre:

> TAXI: I feel like a side 'o slaw strewn across a soggy paper plate.
> DOLORES: These hard-boiled similes get pretty thin. As thin as the skin on a cup of hot cocoa.
> TAXI: As thin as the crust on an East Coast pizza pie.[6]

Clearly Sam in *Gunmetal Blues* inhabits this same world as he remarks on first meeting his blonde suspect: "She had hair like moonlight on topaz, and a mouth that would have sent Shakespeare thumbing through a thesaurus."

As distinctive, generically, as these stylistic features, however, is the voice that produces them. I have spoken already of the distinct differences in the physical surroundings, the social class portrayed, the number and type of characters, and the nature of the action in the traditional cozy and the private eye novels, but not of one of the most distinctive differences, which is the mode and style of narration. The detective, as narrator of his own story, is an almost invariable feature of the private eye genre and is almost as invariably avoided in the cozy. The latter, when it has utilized a narrating figure at all, has almost invariably followed the model of Conan Doyle, whose Dr. Watson, a character whose function essentially is that of narrator, is carried on in such figures as Hercule Poirot's Hastings or Nero Wolf's Archie (despite Christie's radical subversion of this convention in the famous *Murder of Roger Ackroyd*). The modern cozy occasionally still employs this device, but much more commonly adopts a more neutral "God's eye" third-person narrative, with varying degrees of intimacy.

Thus in voice, as in setting, the normal cozy is more easily adapted to stage versions, and the private eye to film. Clearly, when one considers the process of placing a novel on the stage, where even plays with "narrators" essentially present their action directly to the viewer without this mediating voice, the more neutral third-person convention normally found today in the cozy presents fewer problems than the private eye narrative, where not only the dialogue, but physical descriptions in the text, are filtered through the hard-boiled "voice" of the protagonist. One might consider this to be as much a problem in the cinema, which also presents visual material directly, as on the stage, but ever since the introduction of sound, the film has traditionally provided an accompanying aural text, often musical but occasionally spoken, which is technically possible but far less common in theatre. Thus, while no example of film noir provides a continual commentary by the narrative voice, a so-called "voice-over" in the distinctive style of the narrating private eye is so common as to be a distinguishing mark of the genre and to leave its impression, even when silent.

Thus, it is not at all surprising, and surely perfectly acceptable to the audience, when, after the visual cue of the film noir poster, *City of Angels* begins with a voice-over speaking the line just quoted. *In a Pig's Valise* appears to begin, despite its visual evocation of the film noir, in a more conventionally theatrical way, with a live character entering to speak. A few moments into the play, however, the character, Taxi, takes on the convention of the voice-over in a far more radically self-reflexive manner, informing the audience:

One more thing. When I face front and talk to you this way—
this way! This is the Voice Over voice. The big VO. When you
earn your PI license, they issue you your own VO. Don't let it
slow you down. Just pretend that my lips don't move and that
you can hear my voice surple out over the PA all muffled and
crunkly. I'm supposed to be thinking, see.
(He snuffs one cigarette.)
But what I'm really doing is passing on vital exposition as we
make an incomplete transition from pulp to performance. In
other words, if I didn't tell you, you'd never know.
(Beat.)
It's gotta be how it's gotta be. We're all prisoners of genre.[7]

Having been established not as a transparent narrative device
but as a kind of bizarre personal/professional tic, the voice-over
thus enters the consciousness of the fictive world itself. Not only
does Taxi use it self-consciously, but other characters are aware
he uses it and greet this phenomenon with a variety of reactions, primarily negative. Dolores Con Leche, the obligatory
femme fatale, is introduced by Taxi's line, "An Hispanic hallucination was hovering in the vicinity like heat on a desert highway."
Her response is to question the purpose of this bizarre sort of
comment: "Are you talking to me? And why the past tense,
pal?" Taxi, not at all disturbed by this stylistic challenge, explains: "It's a convention, sweetheart. You ain't supposed to
hear, dig? It's for them. *(Indicates audience)* The big VO. Keeps
'em au courant."[8]

If the voice-over provides an essential, though intermittent,
accompaniment to the visual narrative of the film noir, musical
underscoring is found in every sequence and is, at least, equally
important in establishing the feel of the genre. Not surprisingly,
it therefore occasions similar analytic comment in *In a Pig's Valise.* Whenever the name of the mysterious master villain, Dr.
Gut Bucket, is mentioned, the saxophone provides "ominous
underscoring," an effect somewhat similar to the common
"thunder and lightning" in the comedy thriller. Taxi, who

knows his generic codes, remarks "Hmmm. Ominous underscoring" the first time this occurs, and later explains the convention to the ever-opaque Dolores:

> DOLORES: This weird music was following me and I had a creepy
> feeling about the whole set-up.
> TAXI: Could be the ominous underscoring. Hard-boiled tip num-
> ber one: Trust your underscoring.[9]

Later in the villains' den, Taxi, caught off guard by a sudden
burst of ominous underscoring, complains: "Geez, do you ever
get used to the soundtrack following you all over the set?" to
which the "Hotel Security," Bop Op, replies: "It's like traffic. I
don't even hear it anymore."[10]

Taxi's reaction is not only comic, it is also revelatory of the
peculiar kind of generic self-reflexivity operating in this play. As
we have seen in the most extreme examples of contemporary
comedy thrillers commenting on their own conventions, such
as *Accomplice* or *The Butler Did It*, what we at first accept as a
stage setting functioning in a traditional way, for example as a
"real" living room in a fictive world, is subsequently revealed to
be a "stage setting" in a different fictive world. The basic genre
of theatre is, however, what is always doubled back upon itself.
What is striking about Taxi's reaction is that he does not subvert
the "realistic" convention by speaking the truth denied by the
generic conventions, that he is really an actor in a theatrical
performance, but rather by referring to another illusion, that he
is an actor in a film, with soundtrack and set. One New York
reviewer suggested that a "pop semiotician" like Jean Baudrillard "could go to town analyzing the junk-culture-eats-itself im-
agery of *In a Pig's Valise*."[11] The evocation of Baudrillard is indeed
appropriate, not only because of Baudrillard's thesis of modern
reality as that which is already reproduced,[12] but, more specifically, in the importance given by Baudrillard to such media as
film, precisely the sort of medium that, by technological duplica-

tion of the real, collapses reality into the modern world of simulations, of what Baudrillard calls hyperrealism.[13]

The mechanics of film permeate *In a Pig's Valise*, just as the mechanics of theatre permeate the modern comedy thrillers. These mechanics are particularly striking in one of the show's key songs, Taxi's "Prisoner of Genre," which opens the second act. It declares, in part:

> I'm just a prisoner of genre, baby
> I guess I've found my niche
> I'm just a prisoner of genre, baby
> A lonely captive of kitsch . . .
> I'm just a flat-out flake
> I make out in smokey rooms
> I'm dying for another take
> And living for those zooms[14]

Amusing as this song is, it bears a grim message. The active agents in the comedy thrillers, though surrounded by the trappings of detective fiction, are by no means "prisoners of genre." On the contrary, the most active of them take charge of the conventions of the genre—disguise, loaded pistols, hidden panels, even the theatre itself—and turn it to their own ends. Taxi recognizes the conventions of the genre, but this gives him no power over them. He is taken off guard by the ominous underscoring, the dissolves give him motion sickness. Only the voice-over seems his own, and he calls that a "bad habit," the result of living alone too long. In the comedy thriller, where the detective is often powerless or not even shown, the villain often assumes power over the generic devices, but the villains in Overmyer's play have no more control than Taxi. Their ominous underscoring comes in nicely on cue, but is so far beyond their control that it causes their lights to dim, leading Taxi to remark: "You oughta do something about your underscoring. It's death on wiring."[15]

Generic and film-oriented self-consciousness is also an important feature of *Gunmetal Blues, City of Angels,* and *Nick and*

Nora, and in the first two, it is as central to the mechanics of the entire play as it is in *In a Pig's Valise. Nick and Nora* has several sequences as playfully subversive of generic expectations as anything in the other plays, but they are embedded in a dramatic action that is, on the whole, quite conventional and straightforward. Hammett's original *Thin Man* was set on the "mean streets" of New York, and though Nora took Nick also to the haunts of high society, the gritty realism and hard-boiled tone parodied in *City of Angels, Gunmetal Blues,* and *In a Pig's Valise* also characterized that novel. None of this was left in *Nick and Nora,* which attempted, not entirely successfully, to create instead the lighter and more sophisticated tone associated with the *Thin Man* movies of William Powell and Myrna Loy in the 1930s and 1940s. Film, rather than theatre or novelistic dectective fiction, provided the major basis for reflexive comment, but *Nick and Nora* eschewed the film noir references that abound in these other musicals, stressing instead the elegant but hollow life of the Hollywood film community, which provides the play's setting and general filmic techniques in its narrative structure whenever the actual crime is being analyzed.

City of Angels in a sense combines, or at least develops in dialectic tension, the two approaches represented by *In a Pig's Valise* and *Nick and Nora.* In the opening two scenes of the play, as in *In a Pig's Valise,* every effort is made to evoke the 1940s film noir. After the display of the film noir poster and the offstage gunshots, we are shown a brief hospital corridor scene with the private eye, Stone, seriously wounded and then a flashback to his office, where he and his faithful "girl Friday," Oolie, receive a client, Alaura Villiers. Villiers, the voice-over somewhat redundantly informs us, has "a body that made the Venus de Milo look all thumbs." Dialogue, characters, situation, stress the stereotypes of the filmic genre, and perhaps most striking, the entire scene is presented in black and white. As soon as these conventions are established, however, they are disrupted in a very striking manner. After Alaura leaves and as Stone and Oo-

lie are speaking, we hear over their voices the sound of a typewriter. An inset scene appears with a man typing at his desk.
In a very striking effect, he and his scene are in full color, while
Stone's office remains black and white. As the inset scene appears, Oolie and Stone act as if their "film" were running backward, speaking three lines backward and moving backward to
their previous positions. Alaura also returns, moving backward
into the room, and all freeze.

The man at the typewriter stops, thinks a moment, and begins typing again. As he does, Oolie, Stone and Alaura perform
a slightly different version of this sequence. The typist hits the
same key a number of times, apparently crossing out what he
has just written, and the "rewind" business is repeated, with
the actors performing yet a third variation as the man types.
The audience should by now realize that what began as the
Stone "film" (in black and white) is, in fact, a film script still
being written in the "real" world (in color) by the typing author,
Stine. The "constructedness" of the fictive world of *City of Angels*
is thus emphasized, literally, by showing the construction (and
incidentally by carrying out, in a more radical manner than
Brecht ever did, Brecht's advice that epic theatre be presented
in such a manner as to suggest that at any moment alternative
courses of action are still possible). With generic metacommentary moved to the higher plane of Stine, the writer, Stone, the
private eye, does not need personally to provide such metacommentary as Taxi does in *In a Pig's Valise.*

When we move from the Stone world to the Stine world, we
also move from the film noir world of *In a Pig's Valise* to the
Hollywood world of *Nick and Nora*. Stine, a New York writer,
has been brought to Hollywood to provide the script for a film.
Nick and Nora are drawn into the same world of flamboyant
actors, directors, and producers by a school friend of Nora, who
asks them to clear the name of the director Max Bernheim, who
has been arrested for murder. So close do these worlds overlap
that Stine has a room in the same resort/hotel, the Garden of

Allah, where Nick and Nora have a bungalow. One can imagine that they occasionally passed each other coming and going.

Although the dynamic of creating a text and the struggle for authorial control of that text is the central concern of *City of Angels*, while *Nick and Nora* offers a more straightforward and traditional murder-solving plot, the similarity of process in the author's construction of an action and the attempt of the detective or others to reconstruct an action is, nevertheless, clearly demonstrated in the latter work. In the third scene, when Max provides his version of what "really happened" the fatal night when Lorraine Bixby was murdered, he presents the action as if he were directing a scene, with himself as one of the characters. Thus, we get a sequence somewhat reminiscent of Stine's "creation" of a scene while we watch, done now in filmic terms. Max initiates this sequence, which he styles as a "flashback," with calls for lighting and action, directs movement and camera angles (calling, for example, for a closeup on himself to get a particular reaction), and finally ending the sequence with calls for "cut" and "print."[16] Of course, any reader of detective fiction realizes that a suspect's narration of the events surrounding a murder is very likely to be, in all or in part, a fictional narrative, but traditionally it is to the suspect's advantage to dissimulate this fact and to present a narrative that has at least the appearance of a transparent, unmediated representation of reality. Max's story, on the contrary, foregrounds the apparatus of mediation, suggesting that his story, as much as the fiction Stine is typing, is really not a report but a construction.

The central conflict on the "realistic" level of *City of Angels* is between Stone, struggling to maintain his own voice, and his director/producer, Fidler, who is determined to rework the script according to his own taste and what he considers to be the needs of filmic treatment. Thus, an important part of the generic self-consciousness in *City of Angels* comes from the debates of these characters about the film in process. Buddy Fidler begins, for example, with a metacommentary on the "film's" opening scene:

> Those three shots in the dark, then opening in the hospital, Stone being wheeled in. We never said the rest of the picture was going to be a flashback . . . I mean the main titles, then boom! right into a flashback? That's kicked. It's tired. Flashbacks are a thing of the past.[17]

When *In a Pig's Valise* or *Gunmetal Blues* wishes to make a similar metacommentary on a filmic device like a flashback, it is done, as in the discussion about voice-over, by the characters themselves shifting to a higher "observer's" level from which they can carry on such a discussion. Sam refuses a drink offered by the mysterious female, Indigo, explaining: "I tried it once. I kept having flashbacks." We actually witness such an occurrence in *In a Pig's Valise:*

> TAXI: Days like this made me think I should have stayed in grad school. Then it hit me.
> *(Flashback music.* SHRIMP *is caught in a blinding spot.)*
> SHRIMP: Mitzi's in home appliances now. She's cool.
> *(Music and spot out.* SHRIMP *reels, rubs his eyes.)*
> SHRIMP: I haven't had a flashback like that since Tim Leary and I went barbecuing with Bobby. How do you do that?
> TAXI: How do you do the underscoring?
> SHRIMP: Trade secret.
> TAXI: Flukey ditto.
> SHRIMP: Enough shop talk.[18]

Specific generic metacommentary is much rarer in *Nick and Nora* and, when it occurs, is concerned not with specific filmic devices like the flashback or voice-over, but with the more general conventions of detective fiction itself. It is also confined to a few of the large musical numbers. This is hardly surprising, since the overall narrative approach of *Nick and Nora* is far more conventional than that of the other musicals, and it is really only in the big chorus numbers, which according to the conventions of the musical theatre can move more freely outside the established boundaries of the main action, that a strongly self-reflexive and ludic attitude can be adopted. Thus, in the big production number near the end of the first act, as suspects and motives proliferate, the entire company enters with guns to sing about the strange world of "Detectiveland," which they all inhabit, where "everyone has something they would kill for," and where everyone seems eager to demonstrate that. At the end of the song, they all simultaneously "shoot" the body of the victim, which lies downstage center. A very similar chorus number occurs late in the second act when a witness reveals that the murderer wore an overcoat with a velvet collar, and a Homburg hat. These items point to Connors, the producer, but then Nick and Nora realize that any suspect could have dressed this way to pass as Connors. As confirmation, the entire company appears, so dressed, and dances around the body.

One of the most complex, and certainly most self-consciously "constructed," sequences in *Nick and Nora* is also a company number, an elaborate musical pantomime leading into the Homburg hat sequence, called "A Busy Night at Lorraine's." Private eye fiction has, traditionally, a very different attitude toward plot than the whodunnit. The latter follows a tight, controlled, and generally fairly clear pattern, at the end of which all loose ends should be tied, all misdirections explained. The comedy thriller, which is based on the whodunnit, also keeps its action lines clear, even if they are often calculatedly misleading. No such clarity of plot is associated with private eye fiction. The private eye often runs into dead ends, gets sidetracked, plays by hunch rather than ratiocination, and often solves the case as much by luck and chance as by putting all the pieces together in the right combination. Indeed, pieces may be left over, as is most notoriously the case with the almost incomprehensible plot of Chandler's *The Big Sleep*. "Sure is complex," observes Dolores, as the action in *In a Pig's Valise* begins to be explained. "If you're experiencing narrative motion sickness," the jaded Taxi advises her, "don't let it get you down. It comes with the territory. By the time we close the covers on this one, you won't remember which ends are loose." A bit later Dolores persists: "Listen, there are still a lot of things I don't understand," and Taxi responds "Don't sweat it. The genre teaches us to accept the inexplicable. It's a very metaphysical genre."[19]

Although the concluding scene of *Nick and Nora* offers a conventional and logically constructed solution to the crime, there is actually not much preparation for this conclusion in "A Busy Night at Lorraine's." Having discovered that almost every suspect was admittedly at Lorraine's home on the night of the murder, Nick and Nora decide to put all their stories together to try to reconstruct the sequence of events. What follows is a far more elaborate version of the Max filmic reconstruction of the first act. The first try at the scene doesn't work. Nick and Nora make adjustments, moving the other characters about as if they were puppets or dummies, running sequences backward to try another variation from the same point. Finally they have a coherent narrative, making Mrs. Connors the murderer, and they run it through at a very high speed. "Do you buy it?" asks Nick. "No," replies Nora. They decide to try again, assuming that Connors is the murderer and his wife knows and is protecting him. They try the scene again, as if directing a film. When the murder moment comes, Connors refuses to fire the gun, so they give up this scenario. Any writer of fiction has had the experience of a created character "refusing" to do what the author originally intended, apparently the result of a realization on a deeper, more creative, or intuitive level of the author's mind that this action was inconsistent or inappropriate. Since Nick and Nora's "recreation" is, obviously, essentially a "creative" process, that is clearly what is going on here. Yet this process, although perfectly suitable to fictional creation, is quite unsuitable to the ratiocinative process of detection. It may be true that Connors did not do it, but the reconstruction reveals no logical proof of this, only the intuitive rebellion of his "character" in this created fiction. The real message of "A Busy Night at Lorraine's," beginning with the elaborate reconstruction sequence and ending with the Homburg hat disguise dance, is not, simply, that any of the suspects could have been guilty but that the decision about which of them is to be considered guilty depends not upon any logical process or any tangible evidence, but upon the intuition of the detective.

Sam in *Gunmetal Blues* actually puts together clues and determines who killed the developer, Wasp, but the murderer turns out not to be any of the several characters played by the blond woman or by Buddy Toupee, the pianist, but Buddy Toupee himself, the framing character who also exists in the world of the audience. Thus, in order to solve the crime, Sam has to step outside the narrative world in order to accuse the show's accompanist, who shrewdly left the body of his victim behind in the narrative world, like the diabolically clever Puckeridge in *The Real Inspector Hound.* The solving of the crime leaves Sam in something of a generic, as well as an epistemological, problem. Who is to arrest and punish Buddy Toupee in his current reality, and perhaps equally important, how can the musical have a closing number if the accompanist is arrested? Fortunately, Sam is in sympathy with the removal of the rapacious Wasp and decides to leave Buddy in freedom. Buddy is thus able to accompany Sam and his girl, Jenny, in the spirited reprise of "Bon voyage, mon voyeur" that ends the show.

The far less imaginative Stone, in *City of Angels,* is (perhaps mercifully) not endowed with the narrative imagination of Sam or of Nick and Nora, and he is even further from Taxi's vision of the ultimate uncomprehensibility and arbitrariness of the universe he inhabits in *In a Pig's Valise.* But if Stone seems to have no access to generic self-consciousness, either regarding his participation in private eye fiction or in the operations of the film noir, such self-consciousness is readily available elsewhere, on the "realistic" level of this play. Here Stone's world is continually being created, rearranged, and reorganized, since a few strokes of a typewriter can create, destroy, or change any element in it. When Fidler's wife, Carla, expresses concern about the motivation of the two thugs in the script, Stine informs her that he agrees and has already introduced a change. Immediately, we switch to an interchange with "Big Six" telling Stone about the new motivation, to which Carla responds, "That's better. I like that."[20]

The appearance of both author and the characters in process in *City of Angels* may recall Fred Carmichael's *Out of Sight—Out of Murder* or Pirandello's *Six Characters*, but the structure and relationship of levels of reality is very different, at least in the early part of the play. In Carmichael and Pirandello, the still unformed "characters" invade the world of the creator at the very beginning of the action, demanding a hearing and an embodiment in a fictive text. Stone, Oolie, and the rest make no such demands on Stine. Their universe runs parallel to his, and their roles and actions are secure within it. Like Taxi, they are prisoners of genre, but they remain unaware of this. They enjoy the fulfillment sought in vain by Pirandello's "characters"—the fixity and predictability of their roles and relationships within the genre.[21]

This is not to say that there is no interpenetration of the "illusory" world of Stone and the "real" world of Stine. As the action of the two worlds develops, it becomes clear that Stine's fictional characters reflect not only the stock types of the genre, but, often in ways of which he is only partly aware, the people around him. The first clear indication of this is in the sixth scene, where after a tense scene between Stine and his wife, Gabby, (with Stone and Oolie frozen in another set) Stone and Stine simultaneously depart, and the two discouraged women, each in her own set, sing a duet, "What you don't know about women could fill a whole shelf of books."

In later scenes, this convergence of worlds becomes more pronounced, emphasized by the fact that certain actors play charac-

ters in both. In his introduction to the play, Larry Gelbart
suggests some of the variations of this device:

> In some instances, we first meet someone in the screenplay, say
> Alaura Kingsley, and later discover the model for the character
> when the same actress appears as Buddy Fidler's wife, Carla
> Haywood. We reverse the process by introducing Fidler himself,
> oozing fake charm, in Stine's life before revealing him in Stine's
> screenplay depicted as an equally odious studio boss, Irwin S.
> Irving, a man with absolutely no charm at all, real *or* fake. It is
> our way of demonstrating how artists reward and/or punish the
> people in their private lives by the manner in which they portray
> them in their public works.[22]

Certainly Stine attempts to use his fictional world to even
scores, most notably when Stone finds his girl, Bobbi, (played
by the same actress who plays Stine's wife, Gabby) in bed with
Irving, the producer who is trying to take over Stine's script.
Irving is punished for his presumption by being shot, and Bobbi
(after a scene in which Gabby accuses Stine of prostituting his
talent) ends up as a literal prostitute. Neither his script nor his
life is completely under Stine's control, however. It is Fidler who
dictates the casting of his own wife as Alaura, his mistress as
Alaura's missing stepdaughter whom Stone is seeking, and an
old friend as Munoz, Stone's enemy on the police force. And
though Stine uses Donna, Fidler's secretary, as the simple
minded Oolie in his story, he finds when he begins an affair
with her that, in author Gelbart's words, "She's not his creation.
She's her own."[23]

At the end of the first act, *City of Angels* begins to develop a
more complex relationship between its previously clearly sepa-
rated worlds of "reality" and "fiction." Stone, for the first time,
breaks out of his story and moves into a level of awareness like
that of Taxi or one of Pirandello's "characters," directly challenging Stine, his creator. The crisis is precipitated by the play's
central conflict, between Stine and Fidler. In Stine's script, when
Stone is suspected of killing Irwin S. Irving in Bobbi's bedroom,

no charges are pressed, to avoid a scandal. Stone's fellow cop, Munoz, feels the white establishment is covering for each other:

> There're no God damn lumps for gringos. You want lumps? Be brown, be black, be yellow. Everything's smooth for you milky bastards. Kicked off the force. They don't even muss your hair. This happens to me, they hang me by my clockweights. . . . You had it all. The badge. The right color skin.[24]

In the following scene, Fidler demands that "all this 'my' people, 'your' people, social crap" be removed, not only for the peace of mind of the white patron in his "comfy balcony" but even more for the congressmen combing Hollywood for suspected reds and eager to blacklist authors for this sort of social comment. "Change all that brown, black and yellow to red, white and blue," he demands. When Stine protests that such concerns gave depth to his narrative and, more practically, that they motivated Munoz's anger at Stone, Fidler has a ready answer: Munoz loved Bobbi, too, and was driven "psycho" by jealousy. "That's garbage," protests Stine, but Fidler insists: "Polish it! Make it shine!"[25]

Thus, in the next scripted scene, when Munoz challenges Stone, "You had it all. The badge. The right color skin," the lights come up on Stine at his typewriter. He X's out a line, Munoz moves backward and begins again "You had it all. The badge. *(Beat)* Bobbi. Seeing what she saw in you, that was hard enough. What killed me was the way she looked right through me to see it."

This betrayal is too much even for the hitherto unflappable Stone. As Munoz continues to speak, Stone turns from him to look in disbelief (for the first time) at Stine. "You're going to cave in?" Stone challenges his creator. "Just like that?" This leads to a duet, "You're nothing without me," in which author and character vie over which provides the ground for the other's existence. Finally, Stine seizes control by resuming typing and reactivating Munoz, who punches Stone in the stomach, sending him to his knees.

> (STONE *stares at* STINE, *a character betrayed.*)
> STONE: You bastard! (STINE, *ignoring him, types four letters*)
> STINE: "Fade . . ." *(types three more letters)* "Out!"

The lights in the Stone scene obediently follow Stine's directions, and he is left alone, to conclude the song (and the act) triumphantly: "You're nothing without me, Without me you're nothing at all."[26]

Often, in the ludic world of postmodern experimentation, a created work seems to be struggling to free itself from the control of its creator and to gain some measure of autonomy. Despite the many ingenious postmodern experiments in the field of narrative fiction, this project can only remain an illusion. The writer of such fiction can create, at the most extreme, examples of what Eco has called "open signal textures," inviting the reader to provide a content,[27] but this simply shifts an important measure of authorial control from the writer to the reader. The nature of narrative fiction obviously does not allow for any such control to be spontaneously generated by the created work. The case is different in theatre, since a "character," once created, in fact does take on a more independent "life" of its own, the life of performance. Although this independence has been strongly resisted by many authors (most notably in recent years by Samuel Beckett), it is, nevertheless, a fact of the theatrical apparatus and a powerful lever for the destabilization (or even the pretended destabilization) of that apparatus. We have already seen this dynamic at work in the metatheatrical games played in such recent comedy thrillers as *Accomplice,* and Stone's attempted "revolt" from his creator at least raises the possibility of a similar emancipation of the work as a whole from the traditional governing imagination of the author.

The second act of *City of Angels* carries this destabilization much further. After the crushing of his attempted rebellion at the end of the first act, Stone seems resigned to accept docilely the manipulations of his author, and he moves unquestioningly through a series of scenes, as he did in the first act. At times, as when two thugs tie Stone in a shed surrounded by dynamite about to explode, Stine and others are watching and commenting on these scenes, but even then Stone remains entirely within the fiction. A hint of a different relationship is given by Stine's wife, Gabby, midway through the act, who berates him for selling out his talent:

> God knows you're fooling yourself. You think making Stone a hero allows you to act like anything *but* one. If you want to write Hollywood endings, what about one for us, where you start acting like he does, and he writes like you do.[28]

Yet, despite Gabby's irritation with him and Buddy's continuing meddling with the script, Stine's desire to make the film keeps him from protesting, even when a popular Hollywood crooner, whose music has provided background for several of the earlier scenes, appears on the set as Buddy's choice for Stone.

This final outrage may be accepted by Stine, but not by the dispossessed Stone, who, unseen by anyone else, now appears at Stine's side and begins to berate him, in typical hard-boiled style:

> What is this, a joke? Who's ever going to take me—*or* you— seriously again? A *crooner*? Playing me? A tenor I wouldn't give you two fives for? Guess they couldn't get Betty Hutton, right?[29]

Stine seems unmoved, but Stone has had his effect. When the next of Buddy's "improvements" to his script is spoken, he calls, "Cut!" stopping the filming, to everyone's horror. The enraged Buddy orders him off the set and, when Stine does not go, calls in the studio cops—the two "thugs" from the dynamite scene. Clearly Stine is no match for these adversaries in the "real" world, but Stone sees another possibility:

> STONE: Belt 'em!
> STINE: Me??
> STONE: They're not tough. *(Sitting at the typewriter)* Except in your mind. Start using it! *(So saying, he begins typing.* STINE, *thus activated, dispatches the* COPS *using his fists, feet, the clapperboard, and make-up powder-puffs)*[30]

The most striking phrase in this sequence is the stage direction "thus activated." The roles have been reversed, with Stone at the typewriter providing the "authority" for Stine's actions and, thus, for his surprising victory over the "cops" (just as author Stine gave character Stone an equally unlikely victory over these same two "thugs" in the previous encounter). To make the reversal in subject/object positions absolutely clear, Stone, at the typewriter, twice X's out directions, with the same effect Stine achieved by this process at the beginning of the play—all other characters, Stine included, walk and talk backward to an earlier position and take an adjusted line of action. Stine and Stone then sing a reprise of their act one finale, though now from a real position of equality: "I'm nothing without you."

Although, as we have seen, a shifting of material, situation, and even characters from the world of "reality" to the world of "fiction," or vice versa, is not at all uncommon in the highly self-conscious world of the comedy thriller, *City of Angels* still represents a very special development of this strategy. I know of no other play in which an "author" and a "character" literally exchange places, in terms of who is "writing" whom. The only other situation that in some ways suggests this is the sequence near the end of Stoppard's *The Real Inspector Hound* when the two "reviewers," who have been drawn into the world of the mystery play they are watching, are murdered in that world. After his colleague, Birdboot, is shot, Moon rushes onto the stage as well, and when he turns to return to his seat in the audience, he finds it occupied. He and Birdboot have been replaced in the "real" world by two characters from the play, the inspector and Simon, one of the suspects. Clearly, they have taken over not only the space but the functions of the critics, as they exchange the same sort of clichéd criticisms as their predecessors:

> SIMON: To say that it is without pace, point, focus, interest, drama, wit, or originality is to say simply that it does not happen to be my cup of tea.[31]

This situation may seem to parallel the subject/object reversal at the end of *City of Angels*, but there is a crucial difference in terms of authority and of the type of control involved. When a "character" takes over the role of a "critic," he takes over an important (though not exclusive) element in the interpretation of the action—important because the critic's review may have a considerable effect on future reception, but not exclusive because audiences may not read or not accept the review's interpretation. In any case, only reception is involved. Hound and Simon, as critics, have no actual control over what happens to Birdboot and Moon in the play; they can only comment upon it. When a "character" takes over the role of an "author," however, he places himself in the position of gaining ontological control of the fictive universe. He then becomes its "creator" and its authoritative ground. This reversal is thus considerably more radical and more destabilizing than the structurally similar one in *The Real Inspector Hound*.

Having gained the freedom and power of the subject position, Stone realizes that one more sequence is necessary. He returns to the typewriter and announces, "A Hollywood ending!" He then types away, creating such an ending. As the music continues, the giant doors at the rear of the sound stage open to admit Gabby, who joins Stone and Stine to the cheers of the rest of the company. They all three climb onto the camera crane platform to be lifted high above the rest of the cast for the concluding tableau. Gabby's "Hollywood ending" has been literally realized—

Stine has started acting like Stone, and Stone has started writing like Stine. All the trappings of a traditional happy ending are present—the chorus joined in triumphant song, the lovers soaring off above them, united in a final apotheosis. It is, at the same time, a happy ending of a particularly postmodern kind, achieved only by "reality" and "fictionality" switching roles, by the reversal of subject and object positions between "text" and "creator," and by the most self-conscious foregrounding of generic conventions of closure. Both literally and figuratively, the "machinery" of the final tableau is brought out into the open.

9 DEATHTRAPS

PAMELA: **It is not without a sad tear of farewell that you bid a "bon voyage"** . . .
RUPERT: **. . . to your basic one-set, two-act, four-scene, four-actor Thriller** . . .
NATALIA: **Where blood is paint and blades retract and no death is final until the final curtain.**

—*Accomplice*

Clearly, the mechanics of closure present a particular problem for a genre devoted to the subversion of generic expectations. The ending of the traditional detective drama is as highly coded as the events leading up to it. The detective, having gathered the physical evidence and queried the suspects and witnesses, normally assembles the suspects together and, by a physical or verbal reconstruction of the crime, demonstrates which of them committed the destabilizing murder. The exposed murderer very often authenticates this account by confessing, by seeking (ineffectively) to flee, or, occasionally, by committing suicide. In any case, the disorder that has entered the Edenic community is exposed and purged by the logical prowess of the savior detective, and a rational and benevolent order is restored. If there is a pair of young lovers in the play, the murder has very likely interrupted their coming together—one or the other being a suspect—and the solution removes this barrier, so that the restoration of order can also incorporate the traditional comedic *gamos.*

Comedy thriller authors have sought to provide conclusions that will satisfy an audience's expectation of a final appropriate twist or turn, without offering the sort of stabilizing and orderly conclusion of the traditional mystery play, a conclusion that would hardly be acceptable here. The most appropriate conclusion might seem one that, in fact, specifically denies closure, that leaves open the major ambiguities of the play, but this option has been rarely employed. The game of reality and illusion is central to many plots and specific situations in the fictive worlds of these plays, but normally by the final curtain the audience knows which is which, even when some, or all, of the characters themselves remain in the dark. There are occasional exceptions to this, however, as, for example, in *Murder by the Book*, where the audience is kept guessing throughout the action about whether the mystery writer, Selwyn, has really plotted his wife's death or is simply collecting data for a new novel. Eventually, the question turns on whether some pills he obtained are poison or harmless. As the play draws to a close, Imogen, the threatened wife, surreptitiously puts the pills in the drinks of Selwyn and of his sometime accomplice, John. Soon after, she reveals to Selwyn that she does not plan to read his new book since she already knows its plot:

> SELWYN: Are you sure? Was it all a hoax, or did I really try to poison you?
> IMOGEN: I don't need the book to know that.
> SELWYN: You sound very sure of yourself. (SELWYN *and* JOHN *drink*)

IMOGEN: I am. Or I shall be in a few seconds. (SELWYN *and* JOHN
look at her as she holds up the bottle of pills) Yes, darlings. The
original tablets. *(They look at their drinks, then at each other)* You
should be going any minute now. (IMOGEN *imitates* SELWYN
looking at his watch at the end of Act II, Scene 1, *as the* CURTAIN
falls)[1]

As the stage direction points out, the curtain line and final gesture consciously echo the line and gesture given by Selwyn early
in the play when he put harmless tablets in his wife's drink that
he may or may not have thought were poison. The final situation
is clearly coded as a symmetrical revenge, but the stakes are
unknown. If Selwyn truly tried to poison his wife, then he is
now repaid in kind. If he were merely engaging in a cruel practi-
cal joke, then that also is being replayed. Imogen will soon discover the truth, but the audience is left to speculate, as in the
conclusion of the classic short story, "The Lady or the Tiger."

In only two of these plays, *Dead Wrong* and *Deadly Nightcap*,
does a fairly conventional detective follow a fairly conventional
investigation, and in both of these plays he decides, at the end,
to refrain from revealing the truth about what has happened.
In each case the decision is a fully sympathetic one, but it has
disturbing implications. Detective Sergeant Scott in *Dead Wrong*,
investigating the disappearance and possible murder of Allen,
at one point suggests that one does not become a criminal suddenly, but that the moral fabric gradually frays. "The Monsignor
who used to visit my school," he suggests as illustration, "said
that the road to hell is paved with ashtrays stolen from the
Holiday Inn."[2] Allen is not dead, though Peggy's husband,
Craig, suspecting Peggy and Allen are lovers, has led her to
believe that he has murdered him and tortures her with the
details. Finally, she is driven to try to kill her husband but mis-
takenly shoots Allen, who has unexpectedly returned. Scott arrives soon after and arrests Craig for the murder. Left alone
with Peggy, he hints that he knows what really happened. When

he considers ordering a paraffin test for the powder residue, Peggy asks its purpose. He replies:

> It establishes without any doubt at all who fired the gun. It's a very accurate forensic test we have. (*There is a long, long, long pause.* SCOTT *decides*) Which in an obvious case like this, I won't need. (*Pause;* SCOTT *considers, ruefully*) I think I just stole an ashtray from the Holiday Inn.[3]

The echo is an amusing one and makes a deft addition to the curtain line, but it has a dark edge, a conscious acceptance by the detective of the world of illusion and misdirection, which, according to his own moral code, is always entered by just such apparently benign activities.

Deadly Nightcap presents an even more subversive case, a detective who pursues his investigations, does not solve the murder, and leaves the profession to take up another career, that of crime writer. In this new career, he returns to the unsolved crime and writes a short story about it, "solving" it as an author, not a detective. Again the situation involves a persecuted wife, this time one who, in his "solution," is an accomplice in her villainous husband's murder. After she confesses that his solution is correct, he destroys the manuscript and expresses his need for her. She agrees to go away with him, and the play ends with their embrace and with the provocative stage direction: "*A strange look flickers across Sarah's face as Cliff gently takes her in his arms.*"[4] What are we to make of this "strange look?" Is it triumphant? Resigned? Amused? Whatever it is, it surely underscores the peculiar tonality of this ending where, as in *Dead Wrong*, the detective, traditionally the dispassionate seeker of truth, seems to be eclipsed by another familiar type from the detective narrative repertoire, the rather naive young lover, who knowingly suppresses evidence as a result of his romantic inclinations.

In most of these plays, the police, the traditional symbol of order in such plays, do not even appear. Their arrival is frequently signaled by some offstage noise just before the final curtain—a distant siren is heard or the police are heard banging at the door (as in *Murder among Friends*, *Sleuth*, or *Stage Struck*). Sometimes they are being telephoned as the curtain falls *(Double Double)*. Sometimes they have not yet even been summoned as the play ends, though we assume that the closing events will have to eventually involve them. In almost all of these alternatives, we can anticipate that when the police do arrive, they will incorrectly interpret what has happened, and in any case, their interpretation will not depend upon their own insight but upon the "reality" that has been constructed by the actions that occurred before their arrival. This reality is never grounded on some objective truth but is invariably a construct of the dramatic action, the result of some character's careful planning or of some unforeseen (but always highly ironic) accident, and this constructed "truth" will clearly rule beyond the final curtain.

What is most striking about the conclusions of the comedy thrillers is that, almost invariably, they end with a death or in the immediate aftermath of a death, and this death is, almost invariably, that of the trickster protagonist. Even when the death is that of another character, as in *Sleuth* or *Dead Wrong*, it nevertheless results in the downfall of the protagonist. There is usually a feeling of symmetry about this final death, since it is closely tied in some manner with an earlier, generally false, death in the play. The finality of death (and these are final deaths, unlike the ambiguous and often false deaths found earlier in many of these plays) might seem to provide the strongest possible traditional closure to plays that have been otherwise, at some pains, trying to avoid tradition. Moreover, the fact that it is, almost invariably, the trickster protagonist who dies might suggest that even though the detective and the police may be ineffective or absent agents of stability, the dramatic universe itself ultimately rejects and destroys the destabilizing murderer, righting its normal operations through a kind of abstract poetic justice. Rarely, if ever, in these plays, however, does the terminal "real" death truly end the process of irony and subversion.

It is most important to remember that the basis from which the comedy thriller departs is the traditional detective drama, in which death is codified in quite a different manner than it has been in most of the western theatrical tradition. Outside the detective or mystery drama, death, which normally occurs at the climax of a tragedy, is considered a fulfilling act, restoring order to a troubled society and even, as in the main tradition of romantic theory, bringing a moment of supreme insight into the workings of the universe. Death plays no such exalted role in the traditional detective or mystery drama. It is involved with no insight or fulfillment; quite the contrary, it is depicted as an intrusion of disorder and instability into an ordered and comprehensible society, and disorder and confusion hold sway until the death act is expiated by the exposure and removal of the murderer. When the comedy thriller places death at the end of its action, therefore, its effect is normally not to provide any return to stability in the fictive world, but to serve as a reminder of the world's continual susceptibility to such grim and destabilizing events.

Even in those few plays where a specific kind of poetic justice appears to be operating, when the murderer's plot turns back upon himself and results in his own death, there is little feeling that the world has thus been purged of such deadly manipulation—on the contrary, the usual image is of a subversive dynamic put into place that will continue to operate even in the absence of its instigator. In the most gruesome example, in *Murderer* when Bartholomew's plot against his wife fails and she brutally kills him instead, her final triumph is to revel in wresting from him his theatricalized vision of the crime:

> You know this really could be the crime passionnelle of the century. I can see myself in the witness box now, proud, aloof, mysterious. All eyes will be upon me as I weave my bloody tale of wronged womanhood, omitting no ghastly detail of the

drowning of my rival, and the slaughter of my husband. Believe me, Norman, I will have what you have always wanted—a true and abiding notoriety.

To this, the dying Bartholomew can only respond piteously and ineffectively: "No. It's mine!"[5] In traditional detective fiction, when the murderer is exposed, he is replaced at the center of the action by the detective, who replaces also the murderer's world of intrigue and unreason with his own world of order and justice. If another figure replaces the removed murderer in the comedy thriller, that figure often, as in *Murderer,* seems only to carry on the same dynamic. At the conclusion of *Guilty Conscience,* Arthur, who has spent the entire play constructing intrigues to murder his wife, is shot by his wife, who is carrying out an intrigue that is the mirror image of one of his. In actantial terms, she has literally replaced him in the dramatic action, committing, we assume, a crime that will not be solved. Even in *Deathtrap,* where the co-conspirators, Sidney and Clifford, exterminate each other in the penultimate scene in a bloody, gothic apocalypse complete with the obligatory thunder and lightning, the workings of the infernal machine they have created do not cease. The projected fictionalization of their intrigues, the play *Deathtrap,* remains as a spur to further plotting, and in the final scene the secondary characters take up the abandoned struggle and exchange death threats as the curtain falls.

Thus, even in such plays of "purposes mistook fall'n on the inventor's head," where a kind of cosmic justice might be thought to be operating, the subversive thriller dynamic continues through and past the "inventor's" death. The world is not purged. Eden is not regained. Each of the murderer/victims just mentioned probably has some understanding of this in their final moments. Others are even more clearly aware of it, to the point of incorporating their own deaths into their subversive plots or, at least at the moment of death, recognizing the subversive potential even in this final extremity and thus turning it to their own ends. Hamlet's dying line concerning "purposes mistook," is in fact specifically quoted, as he is dying, by Robert, the protagonist of *Stage Struck*, though in a highly ironic and self-conscious manner, since he has arranged his own death as the final element in his plot against his wife and her cohort. After leading them to believe that he had been killed, as they have hoped, by a bumbling private detective, he traps them into truly killing him just as the police and media arrive. He dies in a calculatedly theatrical manner, and if his quotation of "purposes mistook" has a distinctly ironic force, the accompanying "deaths put on by cunning and forc'd cause" is strikingly apropos.[6] An equally calculating forcing of his own death is seen in the intrigues of Stone in *The Business of Murder*, who entraps a policeman and a TV writer, against whom he holds an old grudge, with the story that he has killed the policeman's wife and framed the two of them for the murder. Near the end of the play, his story is revealed as false, but he has used it to engineer a real murder, his own, by manipulating the policeman into stabbing him, with the writer as witness. A ringing of the doorbell promises the immanent discovery of the death scene he has staged and its misreading by whomever arrives.

Even when a character devoted to this sort of game-playing is surprised by death, his ingenuity, often at the last moment, finds a way to turn it to his advantage as well as to continue the subversion of truth after his departure. Lefcourt, the director, who accidentally poisons himself near the end of *The Butler Did It* as a result of his own real and fictive attempts to poison Natalie, seizes the opportunity to place suspicion for his murder upon all the other members of the cast, foreseeing that this will generate excellent publicity for his new play. Milo Tindle in *Sleuth*, though he surely does not expect Andrew actually to shoot him in their final encounter, dies in triumph and with laughter on his lips because he realizes that this final, "real" murder will win the "game" he has played throughout the action with Andrew. Milo has destroyed Andrew as effectively as Stone and Robert, who also died, though more calculatedly, to destroy their adversaries. Milo's final words, blood trickling from his mouth, are also the curtain line: "Game, set and match!"[7]

The deaths that typically conclude comedy thrillers are "real" deaths, within their fictive world (or indeed in whatever meta-worlds they have established—the death of del Gatto being equally "real" in the metaworld of *Accomplice*). In that sense, but, really, only in that sense, they provide a kind of stability and closure to that world. But the more normal senses of dra-matic stability and closure, found in most traditional plays (espe-cially in those which, like these, end with death), are clearly not involved here—there is absolutely no sense of a higher order or purpose than the games that have been played, no likelihood of an improved social order, and if a deeper understanding of the universe is gained, it is of a universe that, like the protagonist, delights in disorder, deception, irony, and chance. The endless play of this universe, as in much postmodern expression, skates lightly over the abyss. When the games are truly over and the final illusions played out, what is left at the bottom may be far more chilling than amusing. The final image of the first modern comedy thriller, Shaffer's *Sleuth*, suggests the universe that the ingenuity and frantic activity of these constructions has only partly hidden, the universe of the mechanical clown, activated by accident, that continues laughing, hysterically and meaning-lessly, as the curtain falls.

NOTES

1. The Business of Murder

1. It is also used, in a somewhat tongue-in-cheek fashion, by even more marginal groups. As I write this, in the fall of 1991, the two most recent examples I have seen of the term are by the New York sexually oriented performance artist Annie Sprinkle, who has called her new show "Post-modern Pornography," while in San Francisco the "Post-modern African American Homosexuals" offer performances under their abbreviated group name, Pomo Afro Homos.

2. Chris Steinbrunner and Otto Penzler, eds., *The Encyclopedia of Mystery and Detection* (New York: McGraw-Hill, 1976), 147.

3. Ordean A. Haugen, *Who Done It* (New York: R. R. Bowker, 1969), 468.

4. Quoted in M. Willson Disher, *Melodrama: Plots that Thrilled* (New York: Macmillan, 1954), 53.

5. Owen Davis, *I'd Like to Do It Again* (New York: Farrar and Rinehart, 1931), 163, 165.

6. Linda Hutcheon, *A Poetics of Postmodernism* (New York: Routledge, 1988), 11.

7. Ibid., 3, 215.

8. Charles A. Jencks, *The Language of Post-Modern Architecture* (New York: Rizzoli, 1977), 5–6.

9. William V. Spanos, "The Detective and the Boundary: Some Notes on the Post-Modern Literary Imagination," *Boundary 2*, 1 (1972), 147–68, and Stefano Tani, *The Doomed Detective: The Contribution of the Detective Novel to Postmodern American and Italian Fiction* (Oxford: Oxford University Press, 1984).

10. Spanos, "The Detective," 167.

11. Jorge Luis Borges, *Labyrinths* (New York: New Directions, 1962); Umberto Eco, *The Name of the Rose*, trans. William Weaver (San Diego: Harcourt, Brace, Jovanovich, 1983); Paul Auster, *The New York Trilogy* (Los Angeles: Sun and Moon, 1985).

12. Josette Féral, "Theatre and Performance: The Subject Demystified," *Modern Drama* 25, 1 (March 1982), 177–78.

13. Michael Vanden Heuvel, *Performing Drama/Dramatizing Performance* (Ann Arbor: University of Michigan Press, 1991), 13.

14. Martin Gottfried, *Women's Wear Daily*, November 13, 1970, 13.

15. Dorothy L. Sayers, *Love All and Busman's Honeymoon*, ed. Alzina Stone Dale (Kent, Ohio: Kent State University Press, 1984), 5.

16. Gerald Moon, *Corpse!* (New York: Samuel French, 1985), iv.

17. Ira Levin, *Deathtrap* (New York: Dramatists' Play Service, 1979), 16.

18. Silvio Gaggi, *Modern/Postmodern* (Philadelphia: University of Pennsylvania Press, 1989), 14–17.

19. Arthur Kroker and David Cook, *The Postmodern Scene* (New York: St. Martin's, 1986), 9–10.

2. The Scene of the Crime

1. Established as literary terms by Oskar Walzel, whose major work, *Gehalt und Gestalt in Kunstwerk des Dichters*, was published in Berlin in 1923.

2. Anthony Berkeley, *The Poisoned Chocolates Case* (Garden City: Doubleday, 1929), 159.

3. George Grella, "Murder and Manners: The Formal Detective Novel," in *Dimensions of Detective Fiction*, ed. Larry N. Landrum, Pat Browne, and Ray B. Browne (Bowling Green: Popular Press, 1976), 47.

4. David Lehman, *The Perfect Murder* (New York: Free Press, 1989), 106.

5. Tom Stoppard, *The Real Inspector Hound* (New York: Grove, 1968), 17.

6. Agatha Christie, *The Mousetrap and Other Plays* (New York: Dodd, Mead, 1978), 425.

7. Rupert Holmes, *Accomplice* (New York: Samuel French, 1991), 9. The dates given in the notes are publication dates, usually a year or two after production dates, which are given in an appendix.

8. Eric Elice and Roger Rees, *Double,Double* (London: Samuel French, 1986), 1.

9. Bob Barry, *Murder among Friends* (New York: Samuel French, 1976), 1.

10. Walter and Peter Marks, *The Butler Did It* (New York: Dramatists' Play Service, 1981), 7.

11. Richard Levinson and William Link, *Guilty Conscience* (New York: Samuel French, 1985), 7.

12. W. H. Auden, "The Guilty Vicarage," in *Detective Fiction*, ed. Robin W. Winks (Englewood Cliffs: Prentice-Hall, 1980), 19.

13. Levinson and Link, *Guilty Conscience*, 7.

14. Fred Carmichael, *Out of Sight . . . Out of Murder* (New York: Samuel French, 1983), 5.

15. Anthony Shaffer, *Whodunnit* (New York: Samuel French, 1983), 6.

16. Barry, *Murder*, 3.

17. Bernard Slade, *Fatal Attraction* (New York: Samuel French, 1986), 48.

18. Gerald Moon, *Corpse!* (New York: Samuel French, 1985), 17.

19. Bernard Slade, *An Act of the Imagination* (New York: Samuel French, 1988), 86.

20. Slade, *Fatal*, 11.

21. Ibid., 49–50.

22. Simon Gray, *Stage Struck* (New York: Samuel French, 1979), 19.

23. Anthony Shaffer, *Murderer* (Salem, N.H.: Marion Boyars, 1979), 35.

24. Ira Levin, *Deathtrap* (New York: Dramatists' Play Service, 1979), 51.

25. Jonathan Culler, *Structuralist Poetics* (Ithaca: Cornell University Press, 1975), 189.

26. Ibid., 190.

27. Geoffrey Hartman, "Literature High and Low: The Case of the Mystery Story," in *The Fate of Reading* (Chicago: University of Chicago Press, 1975), 204.

3. Among Those Present

1. George Grella, "Murder and Manners: The Formal Detective Novel," in Larry N. Landrum et al., *Dimensions of Detective Fiction* (Bowling Green: Popular Press, 1976), 47–51.

2. Fred Carmichael, *Out of Sight—Out of Murder* (New York: Samuel French, 1983), 16.

3. Walter Marks and Peter Marks, *The Butler Did It* (New York: Dramatists' Play Service, 1981), 11.

4. Anthony Shaffer, *Whodunnit* (New York: Samuel French, 1982), 6, 8.

5. Ibid., 49–50.

6. Ibid., 50–51.

7. Ira Levin, *Deathtrap* (New York: Dramatists' Play Service, 1979), 16.

8. Duncan Greenwood and Robert King, *Murder by the Book* (New York: Samuel French, 1982), 30.

9. Grella, "Murder," 53.

10. Henry Becque, *Woman of Paris*, trans. Jacques Barzun, in *The Modern Theatre* 1, ed. Eric Bentley (New York: Doubleday Anchor, 1955), 59–62.

11. Bob Barry, *Murder among Friends* (New York: Samuel French, 1976), 5.

12. Grella, "Murder," 53.

13. Slavoj Žižek, *Looking Awry: An Introduction to Jacques Lacan through Popular Culture* (Cambridge: MIT Press, 1991), 58.

14. Ibid. 49.

15. Frederick Jameson, "Foreword" to Jean-François Lyotard, *The*

Postmodern Condition (Minneapolis: University of Minnesota Press, 1984), x.

16. Stefano Tani, *The Doomed Detective: The Contribution of the Detective Novel to Postmodern American and Italian Fiction* (Oxford: Oxford University Press, 1984), 113.

17. Roland Barthes, *The Pleasure of the Text,* trans. Richard Miller (New York: Noonday, 1975), 16–18.

18. Francis Durbridge, *Suddenly at Home* (London: Samuel French, 1973), 3.

19. Not the reader, since *Sleight of Hand* has not been published. Manuscript copies are also not available, so the comments on this play, as on the recently opened *Nick and Nora,* have not been checked against a written text but are based on notes taken at the original Broadway performances.

20. Since, as already noted, no printed text is available for this play, quoted lines are based on memory or theatre notes and may not be totally accurate.

21. Quoted in Glenn Collins, "The Fun of a Charmingly Nasty Guy," *New York Times,* November 8, 1992, 2:5.

22. Richard Harris, *The Business of Murder* (Oxford: Amber Lane, 1981), 61.

23. Duncan Greenwood and Robert King, *Murder by the Book* (London: Samuel French, 1982), 11.

24. Anthony Shaffer, *Whodunnit* (New York: Samuel French, 1982), 48, 50.

25. Anthony Shaffer, *Sleuth* (New York: Samuel French, 1970), 7–8.

26. John Dickson Carr, *The Problem of the Wire Cage* (New York: Books, Inc., 1944).

27. Carr, *The Three Coffins* (New York: Harper, 1935).

28. Robert Champigny, *What Will Have Happened: A Philosophical and Technical Essay on Mystery Stories* (Bloomington: Indiana University Press, 1977), 164.

29. Ibid., 159.

30. Umberto Eco, "Semiotics of Theatrical Performance," *The Drama Review* 30, 1 (1977), 115.

4. Murder by the Book

1. Ira Levin, *Deathtrap* (New York: Dramatists' Play Service, 1979), 7.

2. Charles Newman, *The Post-Modern Aura: The Act of Fiction in an Age of Inflation* (Evanston: Northwestern University Press, 1985), 44.

3. Italo Calvino, *If on a winter's night a traveler,* trans. William Weaver (New York: Harcourt Brace Jovanovich, 1981), 3.

4. Silvio Gaggi, *Modern/Postmodern* (Philadelphia: University of Pennsylvania Press, 1989) and Linda Hutcheon, *Narcissistic Narrative: The Metafictional Paradox* (New York: Methuen, 1984).

5. Frederick Knott, *Write Me a Murder* (New York: Dramatists' Play Service, 1962), 13–14.

6. Ordean A. Haugen, *Who Done It* (New York: R. R. Bowker, 1969), 468.

7. Agatha Christie, *Toward Zero*, in *The Mousetrap and Other Plays*, (New York: Dodd, Mead, 1978), 441–42.

8. Frank Rahill, *The World of Melodrama* (University Park: Pennsylvania State University Press, 1967), 295.

9. Daniel N. Rubin, *Riddle-Me-This*, MS, Theatre Collection, New York Public Library, 1.

10. Jack Popplewell, *Dead on Nine* (New York: Samuel French, 1956), 19.

11. Ibid., 21.

12. Richard Levinson and William Link, *Guilty Conscience* (New York: Samuel French, 1985), 8.

13. Ibid., 84.

14. Levin, *Deathtrap*, 14.

15. Anthony Shaffer, *Sleuth* (New York: Samuel French, 1970), 64.

16. Ibid., 65.

17. Nick Hall, *Dead Wrong* (New York: Samuel French, 1982), 10.

18. Ibid., 25.

19. Duncan Greenwood and Robert King, *Murder by the Book* (London: Samuel French, 1982), 35.

20. Ibid., 47.

21. Francis Durbridge, *Deadly Nightcap* (London: Samuel French, 1986), 48.

22. Ibid., 63.

23. Levin, *Deathtrap*, 24.

24. Ibid., 50.

25. Ibid., 61–62.

26. Bert O. States, *Great Reckonings in Little Rooms* (Berkeley: University of California Press, 1985), 39–40.

27. Walter Marks and Peter Marks, *The Butler Did It* (New York: Dramatists' Play Service, 1981), 51.

28. Ibid., 16.

5. Dead Wrong

1. Tom Stoppard, *The Real Inspector Hound* (New York: Grove Press, 1968), 9.

2. Ordean A. Haugen, *Who Done It* (New York: R. R. Bowker, 1969), 468.

3. Anthony Shaffer, *Murderer* (London: Marion Boyars, 1979), 53.

4. Simon Gray, *Stage Struck* (New York: Samuel French, 1981), 5.

5. Ibid., 21–22.

6. Ibid., 25.

7. *NY Times*, Nov. 22, 1970, 11:18:1.

8. Shaffer, *Sleuth* (New York: Samuel French, 1970), 38.

9. Ira Levin, *Deathtrap* (New York: Dramatists' Play Service, 1979), 26–27.

10. David Fulk, *The Potman Spoke Sooth* (Woodstock, Ill.: Dramatic Publishing, 1977), 16, 20.

11. Francis Durbridge, *Suddenly at Home* (London: Samuel French, 1973), 29.

12. Walter Marks and Peter Marks, *The Butler Did It* (New York: Dramatists' Play Service, 1981), 18.

13. Ibid., 14.

14. Ibid., 27.

15. Fulk, *The Potman*, 16.

16. Duncan Greenwood and Robert King, *Murder by the Book* (London: Samuel French, 1982), 28.

17. Gray, *Stage Struck*, 32–33.

18. Bernard Slade, *An Act of the Imagination* (New York: Samuel French, 1988), 86.

19. Quoted in Gerald Moon, *Corpse!* (London: Samuel French, 1985), 58.

20. Ibid., 39.

21. As noted before, no written copy is available of this play, and so quotations, taken from performance notes, may not be totally accurate.

22. Herbert Blau, "Universals of Performance; or, Amortizing Play," *Sub-Stance* 37–39 (1983), 150.

23. Jean Anouilh, *Becket*, trans. Lucienne Hill (New York: Signet, 1960), 101.

6. Stage Struck

1. Simon Gray, *Stage Struck* (New York: Samuel French, 1981), 15.

2. Ibid., 21–22.

3. Ibid., 28.

4. Ibid., 35.

5. Silvio Gaggi, *Modern/Postmodern* (Philadelphia: University of Pennsylvania Press, 1989), 15.

6. Josette Féral, "Theatre and Performance: The Subject Demystified," and Michael Kirby, "Nonsemiotic Performance," both in *Modern Drama* 25, 1 (March 1982).

7. Sue Feder, "Death on Cue," *Mystery Readers Journal* 5, 1 (Spring 1989), 4.

8. Fulton Oursler and Lowell Brentano, *The Spider* (New York: Samuel French, 1932), 17–18.

9. Philip Barry and Elmer Rice, *Cock Robin* (New York: French, 1929), 85.

10. John Randall, *Reserve Two for Murder* (New York: Samuel French, 1940), 17.

11. Anthony Shaffer, *Sleuth* (New York: Samuel French, 1970), 64.

12. Terence Feely, *Murder in Mind* (London: Samuel French, 1982), iii.

13. Eric Elice and Roger Rees, "Author's Note," *Double Double* (London: Samuel French, 1986), v.

14. Linda Hutcheon, *A Poetics of Postmodernism* (New York: Routledge, 1988), 11.

15. David Fulk, *The Potman Spoke Sooth* (Woodstock, Ill.: Dramatic Publishing, 1977), 25.

16. Ibid., 34.

17. Ibid., 42.

18. Anthony Shaffer, *Whodunnit* (London: Samuel French, 1982), 89.

19. Walter Marks and Peter Marks, *The Butler Did It* (New York: Dramatists' Play Service, 1981), 18.

20. Ibid., 53.

7. The Audience as/for Accomplice

1. Rupert Holmes, *Accomplice* (New York: Samuel French, 1991), 8.

2. Ibid., 10.

3. Ibid., 10.

4. Ibid., 21.

5. Ibid., 23.

6. Ibid., 43.

7. Ibid., 44.

8. Ibid., 60.

9. Ibid., 10.

10. Ibid., 22.

11. Ibid., 62.

12. Ibid., 60.

13. Jindrich Honzl, "Dynamics of the Sign in the Theatre," Petr Bogatyrev, "Forms and Functions of Folk Theatre," both in *Semiotics of Art: Prague School Contributions*, ed. Ladislav Matejka and Irwin Titunik (Cambridge: MIT Press, 1976).

14. Holmes, *Accomplice*, 74.

15. Ibid., 89, 94.

16. Ibid., 95.

17. Ibid., 98.

18. Bert O. States, *Great Reckonings in Little Rooms* (Berkeley: University of California Press, 1985), 205.

19. Holmes, *Accomplice*, 100.

20. Stefano Tani, *The Doomed Detective* (Oxford: Oxford University Press, 1984), 147.

8. Pigs and Angels: The Postmodern Private Eye

1. Michael Holquist, "Whodunit and Other Questions: Metaphysical Detective Stories in Post-War Fiction," *New Literary History* 3, 1 (Autumn 1971), 135, 147.

2. Eric Overmyer, *In a Pig's Valise* (New York: Broadway Play Publishing, 1989), 1.

3. David Lehman, *The Perfect Murder* (New York: Free Press, 1989), 136.

4. Overmyer, *Pig's Valise*, 3.

5. With *Gunmetal Blues*, as with *Sleight of Hand*, I have been unable to obtain a copy of the script, and so descriptions and quotations are based upon notes taken during the production and may not be totally accurate. The same is true of *Nick and Nora*, which closed on Broadway after a very brief run.

6. Overmyer, *Pig's Valise*, 10.

7. Ibid., 4–5.

8. Ibid., 10.

9. Ibid., 17.

10. Ibid., 30.

11. Don Shewey, *7 Days*, 22 February, 1989.

12. Jean Baudrillard, *Simulations*, trans. Paul Foss et al. (New York: Semiotext(e), 1983), 146.

13. Ibid., 141.

14. Overmyer, *Pig's Valise*, 48.

15. Ibid., 61.

16. As already noted, descriptions and quotations from *Nick and Nora* are based upon notes taken during the production.

17. Larry Gelbart, et al., *City of Angels* (New York: Applause, 1990), 32.

18. Overmyer, *Pig's Valise*, 75.

19. Ibid., 81–83.

20. Gelbart, *City*, 150.

21. A more recent drama, *I Can't Get Started*, by Declan Hughes, apparently provides another variation on this theme. The real-life author of private eye fiction, Dashiell Hammett, who has stopped writing in the early 1950s, is challenged by his detective Daniel Webster to bring to life the scenes Hammett is imagining and which reflect on Hammett's real problems. The play was presented in Ireland by the Rough Magic Theatre Company in 1991, but I have been unable to obtain a copy for closer analysis.

22. Gelbart, *City*, 5.

23. Ibid., 5.

24. Ibid., 89.

25. Ibid., 93.

26. Ibid., 103.
27. Umberto Eco, *A Theory of Semiotics* (Bloomington: Indiana University Press, 1979), 243.
28. Gelbart, *City of Angels,* 161.
29. Ibid., 189.
30. Ibid., 192.
31. Tom Stoppard, *The Real Inspector Hound* (New York: Grove Press, 1968), 54.

9. Deathtraps

1. Duncan Greenwood and Robert King, *Murder by the Book* (London: Samuel French, 1982), 51.
2. Nick Hall, *Dead Wrong* (New York: Samuel French, 1985), 55.
3. Ibid., 72.
4. Francis Durbridge, *Deadly Nightcap* (London: Samuel French, 1986), 70.
5. Anthony Shaffer, *Murderer* (London: Marion Boyars, 1979), 94.
6. Simon Gray, *Stage Struck* (New York: Samuel French, 1981), 35.
7. Anthony Shaffer, *Sleuth* (New York: Samuel French, 1970), 68.

A SELECTED CHRONOLOGY OF MYSTERY AND DETECTIVE DRAMAS AND OF COMEDY THRILLERS

(Dates are of first performance, not publication)

1863	*The Ticket-of-Leave Man* (Tom Taylor)
1871	*The Woman in White* (Wilkie Collins)
1877	*The Moonstone* (Wilkie Collins)
1899	*Sherlock Holmes* (William Gillette)
1910	*The Speckled Band* (Arthur Conan Doyle)
	Wallingford (George M. Cohan)
1912	*The Argyle Case* (Harvey J. O'Higgins and Harriet Ford)
	Officer 666 (Augustin McHugh)
1913	**Seven Keys to Baldpate* (George M. Cohan)
1914	*On Trial* (Elmer Rice)
	Under Cover (Roi Cooper Megrue)
1915	**The Last Warning* (Martin Fallon)
1916	*The Thirteenth Chair* (Bayard Veiller)
1917	*The Trial of Mary Dugan* (Bayard Veiller)
1919	*For the Defense* (Elmer Rice)
1920	*At the Villa Rose* (A. E. W. Mason)
	The Bat (Mary Roberts Rinehart and Avery Hopwood)
	Come Seven (Octavius Roy Cohen)
1921	*Bulldog Drummond* (Gerald du Maurier)
1922	*The Cat and the Canary* (John Willard)
1925	*The Fray* (Ian Hay from Edgar Wallace)
1926	*Broadway* (Philip Dunning and George Abbott)
	The Ringer (Edgar Wallace)
	*The Spider (Fulton Oursler and Lowell Brentano)
1927	*The Terror* (Edgar Wallace)
1928	*The Squeaker* (Edgar Wallace)
1929	*Rope* (Patrick Hamilton)
1930	*Alibi* (Michael Marton from Christie's *Murder of Roger Ackroyd*)
	On the Spot (Edgar Wallace)
	*Riddle-Me-This (Daniel N. Rubin)
1931	*The Bellamy Trial* (F. N. Hart)
	Black Coffee (Agatha Christie)

---

*Plays discussed in this study.

1932   *Criminal at Large* (Edgar Wallace)
1933   **Cock Robin* (Philip Barry and Elmer Rice)
        *Ten-Minute Alibi (Anthony Armstrong)
1934   *Payment Deferred* (Jeffrey Dell from C. S. Forester)
1935   *Kind Lady* (Edward Chodorov)
        Night Must Fall (Emlyn Williams)
1936   *Busman's Honeymoon* (Dorothy L. Sayers and Muriel St. Clare Byrne)
        The Holmeses of Baker Street (Basil Mitchell)
1939   *Angel Street* (Patrick Hamilton)
        *Reserve Two for Murder (John Randall)
1941   *Mr. and Mrs. North* (Owen Davis Bradley)
1942   *Hanover Square* (Patrick Hamilton)
1944   *Murder without Crime* (J. Lee Thompson)
        Ten Little Indians (Agatha Christie)
1945   *Appointment with Death* (Agatha Christie)
        Signature (E. McFadden)
1946   *Murder on the Nile* (Agatha Christie)
1947   *Laura* (Vera Caspary and George Sklar)
1948   **Ask Me No Questions* (Lee Edwards)
        The Late Edwina Black (William Dinner and William Morum)
        Murder at the Vicarage (Agatha Christie)
        Rehearsal for Death (George Bateson)
        The Third Visitor (Gerald Anstruther)
1950   *Home at Seven* (R. C. Sherriff)
1951   *The Hollow* (Agatha Christie)
1952   *Dead Secret* (Michael Hutton)
        Dial M for Murder (Frederick Knott)
        The Man (Mel Dinelli)
        *The Mousetrap (Agatha Christie)
        Murder Mistaken (Janet Green)
        Remains to Be Seen (Howard Lindsay and Russel Crouse)
1953   *Blind Mans Bluff* (Ernst Toller)
        The Man with Expensive Tastes (Edward Perry and Lilian Denham)
        Sherlock Holmes (Ouida Rathbone)
        Someone Waiting (Emlyn Williams)
        The Teddy Bear (James Warren)
1954   *Meet a Body* (Frank Launder and Sidney Gilliat)
        No Other Verdict (Jack Roffey)
        The Spider's Web (Agatha Christie)
        We Must Kill Toni (Ian Stuart Black)
        *Witness for the Prosecution (Agatha Christie)

1955 *Dead on Nine* (Jack Popplewell)
      Suspect (Edward Perry and Reginald Denham)
      The Whole Truth (Philip Mackie)
1956 Double Image (Roger MacCougall and Tad Allen)
      The House by the Lake (Hugh Mills)
      Night of the Fourth (Jack Roffey and Gordon Harband)
      Tabitha (Arnold Ridley and M. C. Borer)
      The Touch of Fear (Dorothy and Campbell Christie)
      Towards Zero (Agatha Christie)
1957 A Dead Secret (Rodney Ackland)
      It's the Geography That Counts (Raymond Bowers)
1958 Double-Cross (John O'Hare)
      Interlock (Ira Levin)
      The Key of the Door (Philip Mackie)
      Not in the Book (Arthur Watkyn)
      Something to Hide (Leslie Sands)
      Speaking of Murder (Audrey and William Roos)
      Verdict (Agatha Christie)
1959 A Clean Kill (Michael Gilbert)
      Detour after Dark (Lucia Victor)
      The Gazebo (Alec Coppel)
      Murder on Arrival (George Bateson)
      The Unexpected Guest (Agatha Christie)
      The Woman on the Stair (James Parish)
1960 Go Back for Murder (Agatha Christie)
      A Shred of Evidence (R. C. Sherriff)
      The Sound of Murder (William Fairchild)
1961 The Bargain (Michael Gilbert)
      Guilty Party (George Ross and Campbell Singer)
      You Prove It (Colin Morris)
      Write Me a Murder (Frederick Knott)
1962 The Big Killing (Philip Mackie)
      Breaking Point (William Fairchild)
      Brush with a Body (Maurice McLoughlin)
      Signpost to Murder (Monte Doyle)
1963 Difference of Opinion (George Ross and Campbell Singer)
      Kill Two Birds (Philip Levene)
      License to Murder (Elaine Morgan)
      The Shot in Question (Michael Gilbert)
      Trap for a Loney Man (Robert Thomas) psychological thriller
1964 *Amber for Anna* (Arthur Watkyn)
      Among Those Present (Aubrey Feist)
      Busybody (Jack Popplewell)
      Hostile Witness (Jack Ruffey)
      Make Me a Widow (David Ellis)

SELECTED BIBLIOGRAPHY OF SECONDARY SOURCES

Alter, Jean. "L'Enquête policière dans le Nouveau Roman." In J. H. Matthews, *Un Nouveau Roman?* Paris: Minard, 1964.

Auden, W. H. "The Guilty Vicarage." In *The Dyer's Hand.* London: Faber and Faber, 1963.

Ball, John, ed. *The Mystery Story.* New York: Penguin, 1978.

Barthes, Roland. *Le Plaisir du texte.* Paris: Editions du Seuil, 1973.

Barzun, Jacques, and Wendell Hertig Taylor. *A Catalogue of Crime.* New York: Harper, 1971.

Berkeley, Anthony. *The Poisoned Chocolates Case.* New York: Doubleday, 1929.

Caillois, Roger. *Puissances du Roman.* Paris: Sagittaire, 1942.

Cawelti, John G. *Adventure, Mystery, and Romance.* Chicago: University of Chicago Press, 1976.

Champigny, Robert. *What Will Have Happened: A Philosophical and Technical Essay on Mystery Stories.* Bloomington: Indiana University Press, 1977.

Charney, Hannah. "Pourquoi le 'nouveau roman' policier?" *French Review* 46, 1 (October 1972), 17–23.

Christie, Agatha. *Agatha Christie, An Autobiography.* New York: Ballantine, 1977.

Culler, Jonathan. *Structuralist Poetics: Structuralism, Linguistics and the Study of Literature.* Ithaca: Cornell University Press, 1975.

Féral, Josette. "Theatre and Performance: The Subject Demystified." *Modern Drama* 25, 1 (March 1982), 170–78.

Foster, Hal, ed. *The Anti-Aesthetic: Essays on Post-Modern Culture.* Port Townsend: Bay Press, 1983.

Gaggi, Silvio. *Modern/Postmodern.* Philadelphia: University of Pennsylvania Press, 1989.

Gilbert, Elliot L. *The World of Mystery Fiction: A Guide.* San Diego: University of California Press, 1978.

Grella, George. "Murder and Manners: The Formal Detective Novel." In Landrum et al., *Dimensions,* 37–57.

Grossvogel, David I. *Mystery and Its Fictions.* Baltimore: Johns Hopkins University Press, 1979.

Hartman, Geoffrey. "Literature High and Low: The Case of the Mystery Story." In *The Fate of Reading.* Chicago: University of Chicago Press, 1975.

Hassan, Ihab. "The Question of Postmodernism." *Performing Arts Journal* 16, 1 (1981), 30–37.

Haycraft, Howard, ed. *The Art of the Mystery Story.* New York: Simon and Schuster, 1946.

Holquist, Michael. "Whodunit and Other Questions: Metaphysical Detective Stories in Post-War Fiction." *New Literary History* 3, 1 (Autumn 1971), 135–56.

Hutcheon, Linda. *Narcissistic Narrative: The Metafictional Paradox.* New York: Methuen, 1984.

———. *A Poetics of Postmodernism.* New York: Routledge, 1988.

Janvier, Ludovic. *Une Parole exigeante.* Paris: Editions de Minuit, 1964.

Jencks, Charles A. *The Language of Post-Modern Architecture.* New York: Rizzoli, 1977.

Kaplan, E. Ann, ed. *Postmodernism and Its Discontents.* London: Verso, 1988.

Kirby, Michael. "Nonsemiotic Performance." *Modern Drama* 25, 1 (March 1982), 100–10.

Kroker, Arthur, and David Cook. *The Postmodern Scene.* New York: St. Martin's, 1986.

Landrum, Larry N., Pat Browne, and Ray B. Browne, eds. *Dimensions of Detective Fiction.* Bowling Green: Popular Press, 1976.

Lehman, David. *The Perfect Murder: A Study in Detection.* New York: Free Press, 1989.

Lyotard, Jean François. *The Postmodern Condition.* Minneapolis: University of Minnesota Press, 1984.

Most, Glen W., and William W. Stowe, eds. *The Poetics of Murder.* New York: Harcourt Brace Jovanovich, 1983.

Newman, Charles. *The Post-Modern Aura: The Art of Fiction in an Age of Inflation.* Evanston: Northwestern University Press, 1985.

Porter, Dennis. *The Pursuit of Crime: Art and Ideology in Detective Fiction.* New Haven: Yale University Press, 1981.

Schmitt, Natalie Crohn. *Actors and Onlookers: Theater and Twentieth-Century Scientific Views of Nature.* Evanston: Northwestern University Press, 1990.

Spanos, William V. "The Detective and the Boundary: Some Notes on the Post-Modern Literary Imagination." *Boundary* 2, 1 (1972), 147–68.

States, Bert O. *Great Reckonings in Little Rooms.* Berkeley: University of California Press, 1985.

Tani, Stefano. *The Doomed Detective: The Contribution of the Detective Novel to Postmodern American and Italian Fiction.* Oxford: Oxford University Press, 1984.

Winks, Robin W., ed. *Detective Fiction: A Collection of Critical Essays.* Englewood Cliffs: Prentice-Hall, 1980.

Žižek, Slavoj. *Looking Awry: An Introduction to Jacques Lacan through Popular Culture.* Cambridge: MIT Press, 1991.

INDEX

212   **Index**

MARVIN CARLSON is Sidney E. Cohn Professor of Theatre and Comparative Literature at the Graduate Center of the City University of New York. Among his books on European theatre history and on theatrical theory are *Theories of the Theatre, Places of Performance,* and *Theatre Semiotics: Signs of Life.*